"Feeding those you love is one of life's greatest pleasures and this sentiment rings true on every page of Sarah Copeland's *Instant Family Meals*. In this book, Sarah shows how to build generous, thoughtful family meals that are practical and healthful yet also deliciously indulgent. From classics like breakfast congee to cacio e pepe risotto and simple saag paneer, this book will transform the way busy families cook, with inventive recipes that can be pulled together quickly and effortlessly."

—HETTY McKINNON, food writer and author of three bestselling cookbooks, *Community*, *Neighborhood*, and *Family*

"If there's someone who can convince me to break out the Instant Pot or slow cooker from deep in my pantry, it's Sarah Copeland. Having had her recipes over many years, I can tell you that the flavors, techniques, and tips that come from her cookbooks are top-notch. I trust her recipes implicitly. Also, Turkey Meatball Soup with Macaroni and Kale, Coconut Salmon with Fresh Herbs and Lime and Deep Dark Chocolate Pudding—BE STILL MY HEART!"

—GABY DALKIN, author of bestselling books *What's Gaby Cooking* and *Eat What You Want*

"You can trust the talented Sarah Copeland to help you make the most of your electric pressure cooker! Far from the monochrome mush you may have resigned yourself to, the recipes here are vibrant, flavorful, and enticing. Plus, they have a sensibly healthful focus, making nourishing the whole family that much easier."

—ELLIE KRIEGER, RD, award-winning cookbook author and TV personality

INSTANT FAMILY MEALS

INSTANT FAMILY MEALS

Delicious Dishes from
Your **Slow Cooker,**
Pressure Cooker, Multicooker,
and Instant Pot®

SARAH COPELAND

Clarkson Potter/Publishers
New York

Copyright © 2020 by Sarah Copeland

All rights reserved.
Published in the United States by
Clarkson Potter/Publishers, an imprint
of Random House, a division of
Penguin Random House LLC, New York.
clarksonpotter.com

CLARKSON POTTER is a trademark
and POTTER with colophon
is a registered trademark of
Penguin Random House LLC.

Library of Congress
Cataloging-in-Publication
Data has been applied for.

ISBN 978-0-593-13972-1
Ebook ISBN 978-0-593-13973-8

Printed in Italy by L.E.G.O. S.p.A.

Design by Mia Johnson and
Jan Derevjanik
Photographs by Christopher Testani

10 9 8 7 6 5 4 3 2 1

First Edition

Contents

To parents, grandparents, and
caregivers everywhere, doing the
difficult but deeply important job
of feeding the ones you love

Modern One-Pot Family Cooking

ON THE SAME OCTOBER DAY THAT MY ELECTRIC PRESSURE COOKER arrived on my front step, straight off the UPS truck, my parents were set to arrive from the airport for a visit. I had four lamb shanks in the fridge and exactly 48 minutes to get a hot homemade dinner for six on the table.

I unpacked my new toy, gave it a quick rinse, threw in the shanks, then added some carrots and celery, a handful of herbs, and a hefty glug of broth. I pushed a few buttons and crossed my fingers (can you guess that I barely read the instruction manual?). Exactly 38 minutes later, with 10 minutes to spare, I laid a warming bowl of polenta topped with melt-off-the-bone-tender lamb on the table—just as my parents pulled up to my door. Everyone at the table that night raved, convinced I'd been cooking all day.

I came late to the electric pressure cooker craze. Even as my cooking-world peers were swearing by them, I maintained—personally and publicly (in my three previous cookbooks)—that all you needed for good home cooking was a sharp chef's knife, a wooden spoon, and a few good sturdy pots. If the world needed an electric pressure cooker skeptic, I was happy to play the role. Did we all really need another countertop appliance? I loved bringing my beautiful, heroic-feeling Dutch oven, steaming with slow-cooked pork shoulder, from the stove to the table (and the silent bragging rights that came with it). Besides, I imagined numerous awkwardly shaped inserts to clean, parts to keep track of, or worse: another appliance collecting dust on a shelf.

I was wrong.

This is going to sound bonkers, but that electric pressure cooker has made me a better cook. It's ironic, considering electric pressure cookers are largely hands-off and literally do most of the cooking for you (while you're off doing something else). I don't mean that it made me a more skilled cook or that it helped me understand flavor in new ways. I mean that it made me cook better meals, way more often. Having, and using, an electric pressure cooker meant more warm bowls of weeknight Cacio e Pepe Risotto (page 107). It meant less six-o'clock scrambling and more slurping savory bowls of fortifying Kimchi and Tofu Stew (page 78). It meant impromptu bowls of Saucy Beans and Eggs (page 32) for Friday work lunch, without missing a beat.

The fall that my family first got an electric pressure cooker (like, three years after everyone else), my oven was on the fritz, I'd just returned from a summer book tour, and my husband and I were embarking on another year as two full-time working parents, suddenly with two kids in different schools—and all without a babysitter. And it was cold—like snowing-in-October cold. The kids were growing like weeds (and eating like elephants). We needed a break. Actually, what we needed most were hot, nourishing meals, not moments of sheer culinary brilliance followed by three nights of snacks for dinner (not that there's anything wrong with a stunning snack dinner board—you know, cheese, charcuterie, crackers, olives, and raw veggies for dinner—but I was leaning hard on them). We needed consistently delicious hot meals that didn't demand any bargaining with a certain stubborn four-year-old (who needs to convince a kid to eat a bowl of creamy parmesan-laced risotto?).

That fall, my electric pressure cooker and I struck a close bond, and I wanted to let the other busy parents around me in on this new (to me) trick. What if I could take what I already knew and preached (healthful and satisfying, delicious and decadent-feeling meals and moments with family and friends) and make them *even* easier—so easy, in fact, that there were literally no obstacles?

Suddenly, I was pulling out a bag of dried beans I'd been too lazy to cook and turning them into a tender and creamy dinner for my kids, as well as tomorrow's lunch for the whole family. Then I started doing crazy things, like throwing three whole butternut squash in to steam (it works, but I don't recommend it—picking out the seeds afterward was too much work), mixing two kinds of grains for porridge (jackpot! check it out in the breakfast chapter beginning on page 28), and pretty much not turning on my stove for 3 whole months (except to bake banana bread; some swear you can do it in a pressure cooker, but I wasn't impressed). I tried just about everything in the electric pressure cooker, including cooking with minimal water (beware of the burn indicator); making glassy, flawless caramel flans (bingo! that's in here, too, page 138); and stretching the limits to find everything it could—and probably shouldn't—do.

Here's what I learned:

- An electric pressure cooker is a family-meal game changer.

- Just because you *can* make something in an electric pressure cooker doesn't mean you *should*.

An electric pressure cooker *can* do lots of things—not all of them—it's great. What it's good at, though, it's positively brilliant at—like tender braised meat, creamy beans, and luscious yogurt—making it easier than ever to adhere to my principle of homemade and wholesome most of the time. With our electric pressure cooker in the kitchen, we eat out less than ever, and I'm still able to cook the big-flavor, complex-feeling meals that keep my family satisfied, on most nights in under an hour.

Here's the thing: I *love* to cook, but standing at the stove all those years sometimes came at the expense of other things—namely, spending more time with the people I love most. What did I do with all that found time? I played with my kids more, cleaned out the baby clothes, redecorated my office, starting running, *finally* watched *Star Wars* (yes, all of them), and wrote this book for you!

There are a lot of fancy tricks you can do with an electric pressure cooker, but for my busy family, I need a dinner helper that makes mealtime super simple—like walk-away-and-cannot-mess-it-up simple. These recipes are made for that. In this book, I've focused on recipes you can throw together in this one pot (without dirtying a heap of dishes) and still get a maximum flavor reward, as well as produce something visually appealing (anything too brown or monochromatic, no matter how delicious, will elicit a *yuck* from my four-year-old). I've given you fresh, colorful garnishes that come together while the pressure cooker is at work and that do wonders to take a meal out of

the *made-in-an-appliance* category and into the delicious, restaurant-worthy corner—all with very little work.

In this book, I am not asking you to shape or stack things, or to use your electric pressure cooker to steam something and then clean it out and use it again for another part of a meal. There's nothing wrong with that for folks who have the time, but if your goal is easier, better, faster, more delicious family meals—without a lot of shenanigans—this book is for you.

And—this one is super important—because you can't open an electric pressure cooker to check on things during cooking, it's crucial to have a trusted source of delicious, tried-and-true recipes to turn to again and again. That's exactly why I wrote this book—with recipes tested in multiple pots in many kitchens across the country—so that when you do open yours up, you'll have something beautiful and delicious to serve the people you love most.

I hope these recipes are a big boost to your pressure cooker game and that you're surprised and delighted by what you make from these pages. I hope you return here often for inspiration, guidance, and big, bold, satisfying flavors. Mostly, though, I hope this book helps you get back *more* time with your family—time for doing the things you love, like playing with *your* kids, taking long hikes, dancing in the kitchen, cuddling by the fire, or piling onto the couch for a good movie—without compromising on serving flavorful, nourishing family meals around your very own table.

Getting to Know Your Electric Pressure Cooker (and Slow Cooker)

BEFORE YOU COOK A SINGLE THING IN YOUR ELECTRIC PRESSURE cooker, multicooker, Instant Pot, or slow cooker, read the manual from cover to cover (it won't take long—they're short). Because every brand and style is slightly different, getting to know the buttons and functions of your own particular machine goes a long way toward ensuring success right out of the gate.

After that, take the time to do these two things, which will exponentially advance your understanding of your machine:

FIRST, watch a quick tutorial on your pressure cooker's branded website to make sure you understand your machine's basic parts and the method for locking, sealing, and starting your cooker. You'll also find a ton of visual resources on YouTube videos. Choose the videos that speak to you and watch for 10 minutes, and you'll already be in better shape.

SECOND, and most important, get a pot of beans or rice going, pronto. Don't leave your amazing new kitchen assistant in the corner because you're intimidated by this novel machine. I promise, with a few dry runs under your belt, you'll be able to make any of the recipes in this book with ease. My nine-year-old, who regularly chips in, mastered electric pressure cooking after making just a handful of meals (under supervision, of course!), so I know you and your kids can, too!

Here's what you need to know about electric pressure cookers. (If you're an old hand at electric pressure cooking, skip ahead to the Short List, page 19.)

Six Essential Parts

INNER POT

The stainless-steel insert that comes with your electric pressure cooker is where you'll put all the foods and liquids. Never add ingredients directly to the interior of the device itself. Always clean the inner pot between uses (it's dishwasher safe) and wipe the outside with a dry towel before replacing it, to make sure no water or food debris winds up around the heating element, which can interfere with the functioning of your cooker.

STEAM RELEASE VALVE

The lid of the pot itself houses four essential components: the steam release valve, the float valve, the anti-block shield, and the sealing ring. The steam release valve is a raised (usually plastic) valve on the top of the lid that can be set to one of two positions: *sealing* (locked) or *venting* (open). The cooker can come up to pressure only if the lid is locked and the steam release valve is set to *sealing*. After pressure cooking is finished, you can rotate the valve to *venting* to release the steam (and pressure); this is referred to here as a *manual release* (*quick release* is another common term). It's okay for the steam release valve to jiggle a little when "locked" in either position, but be sure it's fully positioned to *sealing* when you start cooking. It comes off easily for cleaning, which is good practice.

Releasing the pressure naturally allows all the steam to escape slowly and quietly. When you choose to release manually, be prepared for hot steam, accompanied by a hissing noise. Use tongs (to depress the float valve) and a thick towel (to cover the release valve) to protect yourself from hot escaping steam.

FLOAT VALVE

Newer models of Instant Pots and other multi-cookers have what's called a float valve—a small, sometimes colored metal cylinder positioned next to the steam release valve. The float valve has two positions: *up* (indicating the cooker is pressurized) and *down* (indicating the cooker is depressurized and therefore safe to open).

If you've released the steam after cooking (via the steam release valve) and the float valve is still up, use the back of a wooden spoon or metal tongs to depressurize and release any remaining steam before carefully opening the lid.

SEALING RING

The silicone sealing ring fits into a groove on the underside of your electric pressure cooker lid. Its proper placement is essential for the cooker's functioning (unlike slow cookers, in which the lid settles onto the pot without any locks or seals). Before cooking, always check to make sure the ring is firmly seated inside the lid to ensure a good seal. Sealing rings last between 6 and 18 months, depending on how often you use your pressure cooker, before they need to be replaced. They do retain odors, so wash them well (by hand or in the dishwasher) between uses.

ANTI-BLOCK SHIELD

Inside the lid, right next to the silicone cap (which is the bottom of the float valve), sits a small perforated metal cap that covers the underside of the steam release valve. This cap helps keep foamy residues and debris from blocking the valve. Remove and clean it from time to time (see your cooker's manual for specifics), especially after cooking starchy foods like beans, grains, or pasta.

HANDLED TRIVET

Most electric pressure cookers come with a thin wire trivet with handles, useful for keeping ceramic ramekins or cake pans propped above water and safely lifting them in and out of the inner pot when steam cooking (see the recipes for eggs en cocotte, quiche, flan, pudding, and cheesecake). I use the trivet that came with my model for everything, but you can also order sets of 2½- and 4-inch trivets online. Wash them in the dishwasher between uses.

If your trivet didn't come with handles, you can easily create a sling by using a 16-inch piece of aluminum foil folded into thirds to sit under your ramekin or cake pan; use the overhang to take cakes and quiches in and out of the inner pot.

EXTRAS

Beyond the essentials just listed, which all come with your machine, there are three basic cooking tools worth investing in (if you don't have them already) in order to get the absolute most out of your cooker and to prepare a handful of special recipes in this book: **a wire-mesh steamer basket** (for steaming vegetables, soft boiling eggs, etc.), a **6 or 7 by 3-inch round ceramic ramekin** (needed for making things like flan or chocolate pudding), and **a 7 by 3-inch springform pan or a metal cake pan with a removable bottom** (if you want to make cheesecake).

There are all sorts of additional gadgets available for your machine, including glass lids (helpful), jar lifters and jam funnels, and silicone baking pans in all shapes and sizes. Feel free to invest in them, but you won't need them for the recipes in this book. (If you do buy them, make sure their size is compatible with your cooker.)

Five Essential Functions

The newest, most sophisticated electric pressure cookers come with an alluring panel of buttons displaying their range of special programs. Your user manual should walk you through them in detail, but here's what you *really* need to know, and use, for success with the recipes in this book.

PRESSURE COOK

This is the principal function of any electric pressure cooker and the one that is used most often in this book. This button sets your machine to Pressure Cook; use the + or – buttons on most machines to select the cook time, and the Pressure Level button to adjust the pressure level (high or low). High pressure is the default setting for most cookers and the pressure level used most often in this book.

CANCEL

The Cancel button stops all programs and timers. Use this to refresh your machine if you've set it to the wrong function, time, or pressure level, or if you get the burn indicator and want to restart cooking.

DELAY START

Some newer cookers have a Delay Start button (also available on many rice cookers), which allows you to put ingredients like rice, beans, or grains into the pot, select a cooking function, and delay the start time to cook at a time of your choosing (say, while you're sleeping). I find this most useful for porridges that I want to be warm and waiting for me in the morning (just note that soaking the grains will decrease the

cooking time). You can also use this as a vessel and timer for soaking beans for the usual 8 to 12 hours (do drain and cook your beans in a fresh batch of water, though!).

SAUTE

The Saute function works similarly to sautéing on a stovetop, only it is totally contained within a small surface area and done in a high-sided pot. I don't recommend it for, say, making bacon (you'd need to do it in multiple batches), but it's definitely useful for sweating garlic and onions before pressure cooking and for heating up things like tomato sauce (see Quick Pomodoro Sauce, page 173) and before dropping in eggs for Breakfast Shakshuka (page 31). Know that because inner pots tend to be quite thin and heating elements are very powerful, the Saute function can make the cooker extremely hot, and it takes a while to cool down (much like cooking on an electric stovetop). To this end, if the recipe calls for heating the oil in the inner pot first, heat it for only about 30 seconds to 1 minute, just until the oil sizzles, before adding the other ingredients (much longer and the oil will burn).

KEEP WARM

The Keep Warm function will turn on automatically after a pressure cycle is complete and the steam has naturally released. It is useful for keeping warm anything you've just made, of course, but it's also a helpful tool for reheating or simply keeping food warm when entertaining guests and hosting parties.

Safer, Splatter-Free High-Heat Cooking

(More Uses for the Saute Button!)

Great news: your electric pressure cooker does more than just pressure cook! One of my favorite functions is the Saute button, which can be used in a multitude of ways, even if you never lock and seal your lid. The Saute button comes in handy for things like making hot chocolate (page 153). Because of the cooker's high sides, it's also useful for containing the mess anytime I want to cook something likely to splatter (like homemade Whole Mandarin Marmalade, page 169, or bubbly Quick Pomodoro Sauce, page 173). See the Saute button in action for things like Saucy Beans and Eggs (page 32). If you have little kids at home who like to reach toward a hot stove, you might find yourself making all kinds of things (safely!) in your hot pot.

ZERO COOK TIME

This is a funny electric pressure cooker–only technique that allows you to super-quickly cook something fragile, like a thin fish fillet or tender greens, in the time it takes for the pot to come up to pressure. (See this technique in action in Spring White Bean Soup, page 60.)

Cook It Slow

Most of you have probably already used a Crock-Pot or slow cooker. Unlike pressure cooking, slow cooking is designed to cook your food very slowly—perfect for those who love the idea of cooking dinner, say, while away at work or of waking up to a batch of multi-purpose beans that's been cooking slowly all night—ready to dish into lunches and tuck away for meals ahead. If low and slow is your style, watch for *For the Slow Cooker* callouts on recipes in this book to indicate when a recipe can be easily and successfully made with a slow cooker.

Though many electric pressure cookers or multicookers *do* have a Slow Cook setting, traditional slow cookers are still best equipped for that job—so if you have one, use it. The Slow Cook function on your electric pressure cooker or multicooker doesn't work exactly the same way (or with consistent cooking times) as a dedicated slow cooker does. The crucial difference is that when using the Slow Cook function on an electric pressure cooker, you must have the steam valve open to allow the steam to vent; nevertheless, it's still a locked and sealed lid, which allows for even less evaporation than in a traditional slow cooker, resulting in sometimes overly soupy meals. If you do choose to use the Slow Cook function on a multicooker, be prepared to practice a few times: you may need to adjust the cooking times slightly (recipes tend to cook even lower and slower—that is, with less heat—than in stand-alone slow cookers).

Q+A

Where is the best place to use my electric pressure cooker?

Whether you store your cooker on your countertop, keep it on a kitchen shelf, or tuck it away somewhere, when you *use* your electric pressure cooker, pull it away from your cabinets, walls, and any surrounding foodstuffs or pantry items. The intense heat that cookers generate and the hot steam they emit can compromise the freshness of pantry goods and stain surrounding walls and cabinets.

How can I tell if my pressure cooker is cooking?

Once you select your program (in most cases, Pressure Cook) and time, most electric pressure cookers wait 10 seconds to start, then beep and display the message ON. The cooking cycle starts counting down once the pot is pressurized and then starts counting up, often with the letter "L" (which stands for lapsed time), after the cooking is finished and the cooker is losing pressure naturally or simply holding on Keep Warm.

I can't seem to get my lid open. What can I do?

Most electric pressure cookers are designed to stay closed while coming to pressure and during cooking. For safety, you won't be able to open your lid until the cook time is over and the pressure has been released, either naturally or manually; you'll know the pressure has been released when the floating pressure valve has dropped. To open your lid, use the natural or manual (quick) release to release any remaining pressure (using tongs or a towel), wait for the valve to drop, and then try again.

This is also a time to employ the Cancel button if, say, you have to lift the lid because you forgot to add an ingredient. You can do that by canceling, depressurizing safely, and restarting the machine.

If I double the recipe, do I need to double the cook time?

In most cases, doubling or even tripling a recipe will require the exact same cook time (the amount of time you program the pressure cooker to cook for), but the increased volume of food or liquid *will* increase the time it takes your pot to come to pressure and then to release pressure, and therefore that will lengthen your total time. Adjust your expectations accordingly.

For questions not answered here, contact your pressure cooker manufacturer's customer support service.

7 Things to Know About One-Pot Pressure Cooking

LOW PRESSURE OR HIGH PRESSURE?

High pressure is the default setting for most electric pressure cookers. Most of the recipes in this book use high pressure, except those for puddings, custards, cheesecakes, and some eggs, which need a gentler approach for the creamiest results. Watch for these instructions in the method of the recipes that follow.

LIQUID, GIVE OR TAKE?

All electric pressure cookers call for a minimum volume of liquid in order to pressurize the ingredients; this can be ½ to 1½ cups, depending on the make and size of the cooker. Since there is no liquid lost to evaporation during pressure cooking (the steam valve is locked, after all), I like to use a modest amount of liquid so that the finished dish isn't *too* brothy (except when brothy is a good thing). Note that some ingredients, such as the spinach in the Simple Saag Paneer (page 126) or the tomatoes in the Quick Pomodoro Sauce (page 173), create enough liquid on their own to activate pressure cooking without adding extra water.

TO THE MAX: MIND THE MAXIMUM FILL LINE

On all machines, there should be a maximum fill line (usually called "max fill") indicated on the inner liner or inner pot. It's there for a vital reason—never exceed it!

For soups and broths, I try to make the most of my cooker's capacity, but other recipes in this book (intended for 4 to 6 servings) won't come close to the max fill line on larger, 8-quart machines, leaving plenty of space for doubling recipes, if you're cooking for a crowd. Do keep in mind that some ingredients, like rice or oats, expand when cooked—reference the box below for general guidance.

MIND THE MAX FILL LINE ON YOUR COOKERS CAREFULLY

Two good rules of thumb:

For most foods, don't fill more than two-thirds full.

For rice, beans, and other foods that expand, don't fill more than half full.

NATURAL VS. MANUAL (QUICK) RELEASE

Since the point of pressure cooking for most modern families is to get a meal from the kitchen to the table faster, I use manual, or quick, release to release pressure from the electric pressure cooker whenever possible, though never to the detriment of the finished dish. For all things starchy, foamy, or messy, like grains, beans, or simmered fruit sauces, the natural release is the way to go so as to avoid a messy sputtering steam release. Sometimes, as with firm vegetables like beets or large cuts of meat braised in liquid, using natural release allows for the gentle carryover cooking that makes the finished dish *just right*. Also, when you want to maximize flavor and aren't in a hurry, natural release on things like broths works to your advantage. Other times, a natural release for 10 minutes, followed by a manual release, is the perfect compromise. Watch for these cues in the recipes, and mind them if you can—a little extra time, when called for, is usually worth the wait.

GET WITH THE PROGRAM

Newer electric pressure cookers, and some slow cookers, have program settings designed specifically for cooking porridge, beans, rice, or poultry, to name a few. To make the recipes in this book widely accessible, regardless of the make or model of your pressure cooker, I've mostly used the Saute and Pressure Cook functions—with the exception of the Yogurt function called for to make Homemade Yogurt (page 160).

The settings are programmed with suggested (but adjustable) cook times; feel free to use them if you prefer, but know that the recipes in this book have been tested following the cook times and pressure settings listed.

BURN READING

Electric pressure cookers have sensors designed to be triggered by even the most minuscule threat of scorching: unfortunately, these sensors aren't sophisticated enough to tell the difference between burning and browning (one of the few drawbacks of the

GO EASY, ONION LOVERS

Hundreds of classic dishes are built on a foundation of aromatics (like onions and garlic), in fat on the stovetop, until they are soft, before other ingredients are added; this creates savory depth. You can replicate that process in the pressure cooker using the Saute function (not available on slow cookers), yielding almost identical results.

Things get trickier, though, when onions are added raw to soups, broths, and the like. In a sealed pressure cooker or slow cooker, raw onions, shallots, scallions, and garlic intensify in the liquids rather than soften over time. To counter their intensity, I often reduce the amount of onion or garlic called for in such dishes. Chopping the onions more finely can also help, allowing them to break down with minimal sauté time (a perfect example of this is the Cacio e Pepe Risotto [page 107]—the onions disappear into the dish while lending a rounder flavor to the end result).

Onion-lovers who crave a deeper flavor, go easy inside your pot: try onions sliced thinly (raw) or lightly pickled as a garnish instead.

locked lid; you can't check the food while cooking). When the burn indicator light appears, your cooker automatically shuts off. The most common causes are that something is sticking to the bottom of the pot or that you're just a bit shy on liquid. This is why in recipes like the Breakfast Shakshuka (page 31) or the Easy Eggplant Parmesan (page 108), cheese is added after cooking, with the pot covered but not sealed, to allow the cheese to melt in the residual heat (melted cheese during pressure cooking will almost always set off the burn indicator).

If you do get the burn indicator, carefully open the pot and check for the cause; in most cases, the addition of a few tablespoons of liquid will resolve the issue (though manuals will tell you to clean out your machine and start over, and depending on the problem, this may be the necessary step). Reset the machine and continue cooking.

DAIRY DON'T Pressure cooking dairy items or even some cheese can result in a curdled look, or in the case of melty cheese, trigger the burn indicator. Coconut milk and most nut milks (almond, cashew, etc.) do fine under pressure, but most true dairy products should be stirred in *after* the pressure is released. They can still cook further—whether it's melting the cheese or warming some milk after adding it to the mixture—by using the handy Saute function. Covering the pot with the lid for a moment or two also gets the job done.

INSPIRATION AND SOURCES

I grew up in the Midwest in a town with 150,000 people, and one beloved Chinese restaurant, Royal Dragon, which I was lucky to eat at regularly. My babysitter, who was also the restaurant's hostess, took me into the kitchen at the ripe old age of four—where the snap of the wok and the sizzle of garlic and ginger—captivated me. These flavors were an exciting detour from the grilled pork chop and mashed potato suppers of my home life, which were delicious, but not the only flavors I was ever meant to love.

As a young adult, I traveled whenever possible—tasting stinky cheese from a hotel cheese tray in Holland (at the urging of my dad, who gave a prize for the bravest among us), eating Nasi Goreng (fried rice) and knuckle soup on the beach in Bali, Indonesia, with one of my dearest friends and her parents (my second family), who were born there. Later, I devoured pap in South Africa, udon in Japan, and barbacoa again and again on trips to Mexico, one of my favorite places on earth.

Living the bulk of my adult life in New York City furthered my culinary education. Of the many neighborhoods I called home—Hell's Kitchen and Queens were my favorite. I wandered the aisles of Turkish grocery stores and West African markets, befriended exacting Greek fishmongers, spent hours in Lebanese-owned spice stores, and learned which corner bodegas carried the best dried peppers and the most thrilling mushrooms.

All the while, my colleagues in magazines, restaurants, and test kitchens (Kay Chun, Tien Ho, Lisa Kim, Ghaya Oliveira, Mory Thomas, to name just a few)—who hailed from places like Texas, Tunisia, Korea, the West Indies and beyond—taught me about flavor, how to use turmeric confidently (and why I should), how much spice was too much, or not enough, when to slice my ginger and when to grate it, and how to heal body and soul with a big bowl of Kimchi Jjigae (Kimchi Stew).

As a cookbook author, I am constantly calling upon these lessons to bring more flavor to my dinner table—and to yours. It's not only a wonderful way to remember the teachers, chefs and friends who have inspired me along the way, but also a delicious opportunity to teach my children how to honor and appreciate cultures and cuisines beyond our own.

I am not an expert in any one cuisine, nor are my recipes the most traditional take on the classics versions that they are inspired by. I hope you'll find my versions of saag paneer, tikka masala, and red curry shrimp delicious—and good jumping-off points when you want to dive deeper (and when you are, find a culinary expert from that culture, and learn from them). These dishes are borrowed from the many hands and lands that have fed me. I'm so grateful to them all. Although pork chops and potatoes are nice (sometimes), spice is life.

FOOD WRITERS

The following food writers, columnists, and cookbooks (just a few of the many!) are an endless inspirations to me:

Yotam Ottolenghi, Samin Norsat, Hetty McKinnon, Diana Henry, David Tanis, Bryant Terry, Heidi Swanson, Andrea Nguyen, Yewande Komolafe, Tara O'Brady, Aran Goyoaga

INGREDIENTS

Most of the ingredients in this book can be found in your regular supermarket, sometimes in the international aisle. If you want to go the extra mile and seek out highest quality, super fresh spices and condiments (or mail order larger quantities), these are some of my favorite sources.

Diaspora Co.
diasporaco.com

My favorite source for turmeric, chile, cardamom, and specialty peppers, grown and sustainably sourced in India. A WOC-founded company, working with the Indian Council of Agricultural Research to identify and provide ongoing support to sustainable farmers.

Sahadi's
sahadis.com

Find dozens of spices, olive oils, and other ingredients sourced from the Middle East and around the world.

The Spice House
thespicehouse.com

A storehouse for premium quality spices focused on freshness and variety while honoring culinary traditions and experiences from around the world.

WHAT HEALTHY
EATING MEANS TO ME

HEALTHY EATING, EVERY DAY

Almost all busy families need a simple, attainable path to healthier eating. My hope is that this book becomes one step in that direction for your family. It isn't filled with heavy-handed rules or inflexible meal plans. Instead, you'll find vibrant, flavorful, filling dishes that also happen to be nourishing, homemade, and utterly attainable, all thanks to the help of one incredibly versatile tool: your electric pressure cooker (or a slow cooker or multicooker).

Healthy eating means different things to different people, of course. To me—a cookbook author, certified nutrition educator, and, most important, a mother—healthy eating doesn't mean egg-white omelets and 12-ounce glasses of celery juice every morning. Even if I lived alone, that's not what fills my senses and nurtures me most. But *especially* because there are two other hungry, growing beings in my household and a partner who seems to burn calories at twice my rate, I crave meals that are also filling—and wildly delicious. We all need food to build a life on, food that's full of energy, fast and easy to make, and infinitely repeatable.

For my family, healthy means whole foods and whole grains, natural sweeteners (over refined sugars) whenever possible, heaps of vegetables, lots of fiber, plenty of fermented foods (think: miso, yogurt, and kimchi), big flavors, and, ultimately, a deep sense of satisfaction by the time each plate is cleaned.

Yes, you'll find bacon, butter, brown sugar, and the occasional splash of cream in this book. I believe in moderation, and all those things can be a part of balanced eating. But you'll also find bowls of clean, steamy bean soups chock-full of greens and fresh vegetables; divine, deeply hued stewed fruits in place of pies; and good-for-you grains like millet and amaranth to play with, which can help you inch closer to your own health goals.

And even when we are sitting down to a decadent-seeming meal in our house, we strive for balance: breakfast is served with a side of fresh fruit or a tall green smoothie; on our dinner plates, you'll find the meals on these pages *plus* a giant green salad. You can't make smoothies or salads in a pressure cooker, so you won't find recipes for them here, though do check out Salad Helpers on page 27 to learn how one-pot cooking can improve even your salad game, so they can be on your table, too.

6 SIMPLE HABITS FOR
HEALTHIER FAMILY MEALS

EAT WHOLE FOODS

Any time you choose fresh, whole, unprocessed food over something from a package or, for that matter, a takeout box, you're already making a healthier choice. What's important is that you're starting with whole, raw, unprocessed ingredients and, with the fast magic of your pressure cooker, turning them into meals with ingredients your body can easily recognize and convert into energy that lasts.

But what about canned foods?

Yes, canned foods like beans and tomatoes are processed—minimally. But they're also a helpful shortcut for busy families and, in moderation, make a fine replacement for the home-cooked kind (check the nutritional panel for sodium and other additives). Don't feel obligated to spend your whole summer pressure canning your own sun-ripened tomatoes unless that's what you love to do.

EAT MORE PLANT FOODS

Plant foods, be they vegetables, beans, whole grains, nuts, fruits, or seeds, are the ideal source of energy for humans. That doesn't mean we all have to become vegans or vegetarians, but putting more plants—vegetables, especially—into every meal is a very good idea, no matter what diet you subscribe to.

For the recipes in this book, look for opportunities to substitute extra vegetables for some of the meat. See, for instance, Chicken Tikka Masala (page 111), with an option to replace half the chicken with cauliflower and chickpeas—or

go all the way vegetarian with it. Love the idea of more vegetables but need something familiar and comforting? Dive into the Soup au Pistou (page 52) or Celery Root Soup (page 62). You get the idea.

SIT DOWN TOGETHER

One of the healthiest habits of all is sitting down when you eat. Make a pact with your crew to eat only at the table (except, say, once a week when you gather around a floor picnic while watching a movie or a game) and together as a family whenever possible. Aim for consistent meal times—with some flexibility, of course—and watch your minds and bodies (and family unity!) grow healthier by the meal.

EMBRACE SMART PROTEINS

Smart, or lean, proteins can include fish and seafood (try Red Curry Shrimp, page 115, or the quick-as-a-wink Coconut Salmon, page 116); beans and legumes (check out Marinated Picnic Beans, page 84, or the Dreamy, Creamy (Any-Bean) Hummus variation on page 83); eggs (Breakfast Shakshuka, page 31, or Saucy Beans and Eggs, page 32, are good places to start); and chicken and turkey in small amounts (dive into Turkey Meatball Soup, page 69). When I eat heavier meats like pork and beef, I like to serve them with hearty servings of vegetables (see Double-the-Vegetables Pot Roast, page 129, with loads of carrots; or Traditional Beef Borscht, page 72, which is chock-full of beets), so we're always bulking up on plant foods.

When you're going all out on meat (like for Pulled Pork Tacos, page 125, or Quick Pork Bolognese for a Crowd, page 122), serve smaller portions accompanied by a hefty salad, or make them once-in-a-while foods—say, every Sunday night.

DRINK MORE WATER

We all know we should be drinking more water! But water is boring, right? Not so fast. Water-based broths and warm drinks are hydrating and can have tons of flavor! Try a brothy soup like Spring White Bean Soup (page 60), which is both filling and nourishing, thanks to the flavorful broth. Here are a few more ideas: sip homemade Beef Bone Broth, Pho Style (page 176), between meals, or be generous with your pours of warm, frothy beverages like Homemade Chai Masala (page 156) and Golden Milk (Turmeric) Latte (page 154), which are satisfying and naturally sweetened.

EMBRACE MEAL PLANNING

Even with an electric pressure cooker in your corner, dinner doesn't make itself. Set aside a few hours each week (any day of the week) to make a shopping list, plan at least three solid dinners and several breakfasts, and meal-prep for the week ahead (whip up a 20-minute healthier jam for toasts and porridges, simmer some beans for lunches, or set your Delay Start for tomorrow's breakfast bowl).

If the idea of grocery shopping, meal prepping, *and* cooking ahead all leads you to a giant case of overwhelm (I hear you!), consider some amount of online grocery shopping. In our home, we have mail-order subscriptions for sustainable seafood (Sea to Table), grass-fed and organic meat (ButcherBox), and bulk pantry items (Thrive Market), all of which save me a lot of time shopping, leaving more time for making our meals from scratch.

FAMILY MEALS FOR ALL (KINDS OF) EATERS

In our family, we have one vegetarian, one meat enthusiast, three seafood lovers, and two people who mostly avoid wheat. Maybe your family looks a bit like this, too! I don't (a.k.a. won't!) cook separate meals for everyone.

To make the entire table happy, I often turn to cozy casserole-type dishes like Easy Eggplant Parmesan (page 108), or an eggs-for-dinner meal like Breakfast Shakshuka (page 31). A beans- or legumes-centric meal, like Red Lentil Dal (page 66), are also always a hit, as are other meatless soups and stews (with a side of toasted bread for heartier eaters).

On the nights I do serve meat, vegetarians get big grain bowls or salads with reinvented leftovers like warm vegetable bits and Fennel-Roasted Chickpeas (page 64) or a quick, please-all dinner of pasta with Quick Pomodoro Sauce (page 173), which I always have on hand (either in the fridge or stashed away in the freezer).

Make "mix, match, and remake" your mantra, and use the staples chapter (page 158) for shortcuts to make sure everyone is satisfied, without creating extra work for yourself.

BRIGHT COLOR, BRIGHT FLAVOR

There's magic in the vibrant colors found in nature. The big, bold colors of turmeric (Coconut Salmon, page 116, or Chickpea Coconut Curry, page 55); beets (Traditional Beef Borscht, page 72, or No-Fuss Steamed Beets, page 94); and leafy greens and herbs (Spring White Bean Soup, page 60) translate to both flavor *and* powerful antioxidants. The spices in this book can be found in your average grocery store (or ordered online); likewise, the herbs, which are also easy to grow even on a fire escape in the world's biggest city, can be loaded into your meals with gusto!

NATURAL FLAVOR UPS

Here are ten all-natural ingredients (with some swaps) that add tons of flavor to your meals but no empty calories, saturated fats, or artificial ingredients:

- Anchovies
- Citrus zest and juice
- High-quality extra-virgin olive oil
- Tamari, soy sauce, or fish sauce
- Harissa, paprika paste, sambal, or chile oil
- Sea salt
- Miso
- Fresh herbs
- Toasted nuts and seeds
- Capers or olives

SALAD HELPERS

Though you can't make a salad in an electric pressure cooker, you *can* use it to make salads better. Here are eight stunning salad combinations built around components (recipes found in this book!) that are quicker, faster, and easier to prepare in your pressure cooker:

- Cooked beets (see page 94) + avocados + watercress + crumbly cheese
- Shaved Brussels sprouts + white beans (see page 60) + pomegranate + walnuts
- Kale + shaved radishes + poached chicken (see page 178) + ranch dressing
- Soft-boiled eggs (see page 39) + green beans + romaine + olives + tomatoes
- Pinto beans (see page 181) + pickled onions + avocados + parsley + dill
- Dreamy, Creamy (Any-Bean) Hummus (page 83) + Honey-Braised Carrots (page 88) + Little Gem lettuce + arugula
- Heirloom tomatoes + Creamed Mexican Street Corn (page 97) + chopped herbs
- Marinated Picnic Beans (page 84) + chopped cucumbers + olives + feta

SPECIAL DIETS

There are a lot of meals in this cookbook for all kinds of eaters. There are plenty of plant-based recipes, but there are also big, juicy pots of braised short ribs and stunningly simple but satisfying stewed chicken dinners, too. Likewise, the recipes aren't exclusively gluten-free or vegan, but many of them are, and many can easily be made that way. Check the Special Diets Index (page 188) to find the recipes that work best for your family.

EGGS, TOASTS
+ BREAKFAST
BOWLS

Breakfast is our first shot at greatness—a meal that can leave a lasting mark on your family's whole day. I am a big believer in going big at breakfast, both as a mother and as an eater. Yes, some days are grab-and-go, but they shouldn't all be. Morning is the perfect time to employ a little help from an electric pressure cooker, programming it to start the day with something hopeful and nourishing, like a porridge topped with tropical fruit (see page 44), a satisfying Breakfast Shakshuka (page 31), or a steamy bowl of congee (see page 36), while you slip into the shower, pack the lunches, and line up little mittens and boots by the door.

The charm of an electric pressure cooker as a breakfast helper is a powerful one—certainly on chaotic weekday mornings, but on weekends, too. Sure, toast and scrambled eggs don't take that long on the stovetop. But what about toast with a low-sugar homemade jam (see page 167) so luscious you could eat it by the spoonful? How about jammy soft-cooked eggs—the kind you see in magazines—with shells that practically slide off (see page 39)? Or a luscious bowl of Irish oats you didn't have to stand over and stir, topped with peanut butter, chocolate, and berries (see page 47)? With an electric pressure cooker by your side, a hearty, healthy breakfast, any day of the week, has never been easier.

Breakfast Shakshuka
with Feta and Dill

PREP TIME: 10 MINUTES
TOTAL TIME: 20 MINUTES
SERVES 4 TO 8
GLUTEN-FREE* VEGETARIAN

SHAKSHUKA

1 tablespoon unsalted butter, room temperature, or olive oil

3 cups Quick Pomodoro Sauce (page 173) or prepared marinara sauce

Pinch of red pepper flakes

¼ teaspoon ground cumin

8 large eggs

4 ounces feta cheese, crumbled

FOR SERVING

Perfect Toast (see box, page 48, optional) *For gluten-free, omit bread or use gluten-free toast

1 small shallot, thinly sliced

Caper berries

¼ cup (packed) torn fresh dill

Extra-virgin olive oil

Flaky sea salt, such as Maldon

Freshly ground black pepper

Shakshuka, a Middle Eastern dish of eggs poached in a spiced tomato sauce, is one of those fast, impressive dishes that is so much more than the sum of its parts. I make this on cold winter mornings, for impromptu lunches, and even on "eggs for dinner" nights (if you're not already hip to this easy dinner, give it a shot). Perfect Toast (see page 48) takes this over the top, but it's pretty chic all on its own, too.

1. Brush the bottom of the inner pot of the pressure cooker with the butter. Add the sauce, red pepper flakes, and cumin and stir to combine.

2. Crack 8 eggs (1 or 2 per person) into the sauce. Lock on the lid and Pressure Cook on low pressure for 1 minute. Immediately release the pressure manually (to prevent the eggs from overcooking) and open the lid. Check the yolks; if you like a firmer yolk, turn off the heat, re-cover with the lid (but don't lock it), and let the eggs sit for 1 to 2 minutes more, until set.

3. Open the lid and sprinkle the feta over the top of the eggs to warm it. Spoon the sauce, eggs, and feta into shallow bowls or over the toast and sprinkle with shallot, caper berries, and dill. Drizzle with olive oil if desired, and finish with a sprinkle of flaky salt and pepper.

Saucy Beans and Eggs

PREP TIME: 5 MINUTES
TOTAL TIME: 25 MINUTES
SERVES 4
GLUTEN-FREE* VEGETARIAN*

BEAN

2 tablespoons extra-virgin
olive oil

4 garlic cloves, smashed or
thinly sliced

½ teaspoon cumin seeds
(optional)

3 cups cooked pinto beans (see
page 181) or white beans; or
canned beans, rinsed and
drained

1¼ to 1½ cups chicken or
vegetable broth (such as on
pages 178, 174)
*For vegetarian, use vegetable
broth

½ teaspoon fine sea salt

Freshly ground black pepper

4 large eggs

FOR SERVING

Extra-virgin olive oil

Chopped fresh mint

Flaky sea salt, such as Maldon

Freshly ground black pepper

Garlicky Pistou (see page 54)

Perfect Toast (see box,
page 48) *For gluten-free, omit
bread or use gluten-free toast

Never underestimate the power of simplicity. On a winter weekday morning, or even a summer weekend, saucy beans with an egg poached right in the center of them (all in one pot) is a filling, sustaining meal, perfect for the savory set. Add a dollop of Garlicky Pistou (see page 54), or pesto, or any other secret sauce you have stocked in your fridge and watch the crowd go wild.

1. Place the olive oil, garlic, and cumin seeds in the inner pot of a pressure cooker and set to the Saute function. Cook about 1 minute, or until fragrant. Add the beans, broth, salt, and some pepper and continue on the Saute setting to soften the beans until the mixture is saucy, stirring the beans occasionally to release their starches and thicken the sauce, about 4 minutes.

2. Crack the eggs into the beans and cook on the Saute setting until the whites are just starting to set, 1 to 2 minutes. Cover the pot (don't lock), turn off the heat, and let the eggs continue to cook until the whites are fully set and the yolks are soft and creamy, 3 to 4 minutes more, depending on how firm you like your yolks.

3. Open the lid and spoon the beans and eggs into shallow bowls or serve over toast, drizzled with some olive oil and sprinkled with the mint, flaky salt, and pepper. Serve with a dollop of pistou, if desired.

Baked Eggs for a Crowd

(EGGS EN COCOTTE)

PREP TIME: 5 MINUTES
TOTAL TIME: 15 MINUTES
SERVES 4
GLUTEN-FREE* VEGETARIAN

2 tablespoons unsalted butter, cut into pieces, plus additional for greasing

¼ cup light cream or half-and-half

8 large eggs

Flaky sea salt, such as Maldon

Freshly cracked black peppercorns

Chopped fresh herbs, such as dill or chives

Perfect Toast (see box, page 48) or fresh baguette, sliced (optional) *For gluten-free, omit bread or use gluten-free toast

EQUIPMENT: 6 by 3-inch or 7 by 3-inch ceramic ramekin

I learned to make eggs en cocotte in France. These are soft-yolked eggs poached to an oozy perfection in a butter-and-cream bath and topped with finely chopped herbs. I have leaned *heavily* on this easy trick for years, because it is elegant, simple, and truly delicious—and the eggs mingle with the cream to make an instant sauce. You can pressure cook the eggs individually if you have small (2- to 3-ounce) ramekins, but I love doing 6 to 8 eggs at a time in a soufflé dish for the same effect with much less fuss. Serve these eggs in the center of the table, with stacks of toast or slices of fresh baguette, and have a large serving spoon for scooping out the quivery eggs, one or two at a time.

1. Pour about 1 cup water in the inner pot of the pressure cooker. Add a trivet to the inner pot.

2. Grease the ramekin with a little butter. Add the 2 tablespoons butter and the cream to the ramekin; crack the eggs right in, making sure the yolks stay whole.

3. Place the ramekin on the trivet and lock on the lid. Pressure Cook on low pressure for 5 to 6 minutes. (I like my eggs at 5 minutes, so the yolks are jammy and thick, but not runny.)

4. Release the pressure manually, then open the lid and immediately remove the trivet and ramekin using the trivet's handles (they may be hot). Sprinkle the eggs generously with flaky salt, pepper, and fresh herbs. Serve warm, over the toast or with slices of fresh baguette.

All-Purpose Crustless Quiche

PREP TIME: 20 MINUTES
TOTAL TIME: 1 HOUR
SERVES 6 TO 8
GLUTEN-FREE VEGETARIAN*

1 tablespoon unsalted butter

5 tablespoons finely grated parmesan cheese, plus more for serving

½ cup whole milk

½ cup heavy cream

10 large eggs

2 tablespoons cornstarch

1 teaspoon fine sea salt

Freshly ground black pepper

3 ounces Manchego, Cheddar, Gruyère, Asiago, or Havarti cheese, grated (about 1 cup)

1 cup finely chopped broccolini or broccoli florets

1 cup chopped or crumbled cooked breakfast sausage, ham, bacon, or chorizo (optional) *For vegetarian, omit meat or use plant-based meat substitute

1 packed cup mixed fresh herbs, such as dill, parsley, and mint, roughly chopped

EQUIPMENT: 6 by 3-inch or 7 by 3-inch ceramic ramekin or solid cake pan (not with removable bottom)

TRY THIS!
GOLDEN-BROWN QUICHE

If you prefer a quiche with a golden-brown top (the kind you'd get from a traditional oven bake), follow the instructions through step 5. Preheat oven broiler to low. Sprinkle the top of the quiche with another 3 tablespoons parmesan and place at least 6 inches from the heat source until golden brown on top, 1 to 2 minutes.

I wasn't sold on the idea of a pressure-cooker quiche, since I like the brown edges of a classic oven-finished version, but the promise of a set-it-and-forget-it breakfast for a crowd won me over. The result is these custardy eggs, with pops of vegetables and cheese, and zero risk of overcooking or drying out. You can use this recipe as a formula for any kind of crustless quiche, whether chock-full of vegetables (think: asparagus, broccoli, artichokes) or meat and cheese (classic ham and Cheddar, or bacon and Gruyère). Also, try spicy chorizo with Manchego and leftover cooked potatoes, for a Spanish flair. In fact, this is a great recipe for using a flavored cheese, like those made with horseradish or chipotle, or a dill Havarti, to lend extra flavor without extra work. Finish this blond egg casserole with a dusting of herbs—whatever you have in the fridge—and a little extra cheese on top. A cream/milk combination makes the creamiest filling; you can also use 1 cup half-and-half instead.

1. Pour about 1½ cups water into the inner pot of the pressure cooker. Place a trivet or steamer rack in the inner pot.

2. Grease the ramekin with the butter. Sprinkle the bottom and sides with 2 tablespoons of the parmesan.

3. Whisk together the milk, cream, eggs, cornstarch, and salt in a medium bowl. (I like to blitz this mixture with an immersion blender or in an upright blender to make sure it's perfectly smooth.) Stir in some pepper, 3 ounces semi-firm grated cheese such as Manchego, broccolini, sausage, and remaining 3 tablespoons parmesan.

4. Pour the egg mixture into the prepared ramekin and cover it tightly with foil. Place the ramekin on the trivet. Lock on the lid and Pressure Cook on high pressure for 20 minutes. Let the pressure release naturally for 10 minutes, then release the remaining pressure manually.

5. Open the lid and remove the ramekin from the trivet using the trivet's handles. Discard the foil. Let cool until easy to handle, about 5 minutes.

6. Sprinkle the top with the herbs and more parmesan, if desired, and serve warm, sliced into wedges.

Breakfast Congee
with Egg, Avocado, and Scallion
(JOOK)

PREP TIME: 5 MINUTES
TOTAL TIME: 35 MINUTES
SERVES 4
GLUTEN-FREE

¾ cup long-grain white rice

4 cups chicken or pork broth
(see pages 178, 177)

1 tablespoon grated peeled
fresh ginger

Pinch of fine sea salt

4 large eggs, fried or soft-boiled

1 avocado, peeled and sliced

2 or 3 scallions, green and white
parts thinly sliced

Chile oil, for serving

Congee (also known as Jook) is a deeply satisfying savory rice porridge found throughout Asia—and a lush answer for those who crave a warm, creamy breakfast (or anytime meal) that isn't sweet. I've learned to lean on this ancient dish because it's nourishing and easy to make, and infinitely adaptable. Cooking the rice in broth builds flavor right in, leaving you free to keep the toppings simple (butter and salt), or go all-out with pulled pork, fresh ginger, wild mushrooms, or more. My kids love being in charge of topping their own meals, whether it's a loaded baked potato or a warm bowl of porridge, and congee is made for exactly that (see Try This!). Our go-to topping is over-easy eggs, avocado, and thinly sliced scallion (as thin as you can go) but there are very few wrong ways to top your own bowl of congee.

GET A HEAD START

Porridge is the perfect candidate for using your pressure cooker's timer setting. Program the timer at night using the Delay Start setting, so you can wake up to creamy and literally instant porridge the next morning. (You can do the same thing in most modern rice cookers or multicookers, using the timer and the Porridge setting.)

FOR THE SLOW COOKER

Butter the interior of the slow cooker (grains and porridges tend to stick). Cook the congee on Low for 4 hours.

1. Soak the rice in water for 15 minutes (see Cook's Note, page 102) and then rinse until the water runs clear; drain.

2. Combine the rice, broth, ginger, and salt in the inner pot of the pressure cooker. Pressure Cook on high pressure for 15 to 20 minutes, depending on the texture you want—the longer you cook the rice, the creamier it will become.

3. Let the pressure release naturally (about 10 minutes), then leave the cooker on the Keep Warm setting until you are ready to serve.

4. Open the lid. Spoon the porridge into bowls and serve steaming hot, topped with eggs, avocado, and scallions. Drizzle with the chile oil, if using, or with any other toppings you desire.

TRY THIS! A CONGEE TOPPINGS BAR

The quickest way to get the whole family on board with congee is to set up a toppings bar and let everyone garnish his or her own bowl as desired. Use the congee recipe as a starting point, but don't hold back in your quest to find perfect combinations. Try topping the congee with crumbled breakfast sausage, shredded roasted chicken, or pulled pork, sautéed shiitake mushrooms, leftover roasted vegetables, fresh cilantro, kimchi, steamed bok choy, roasted peanuts, or any combination of these.

Jammy Egg Toast

(PERFECT EGGS YOUR WAY, EVERY TIME)

PREP TIME: 5 MINUTES
TOTAL TIME: 15 MINUTES
MAKES 2 TO 12 EGGS
VEGETARIAN

2 to 12 large eggs
(see Cook's Note)

Small pat of unsalted or salted butter (preferably cultured for extra flavor)

Flaky sea salt, such as Maldon

Freshly cracked black peppercorns

Chopped fresh herbs, such as dill or chives (optional)

Perfect Toast (see box, page 48), for serving

COOK'S NOTE

Pressure Cooking Your Eggs: I don't use the pressure cooker for cooking fewer than 4 eggs, though you can. This is the perfect method for uniformly soft-boiling a dozen, or even 2 dozen, eggs so you might as well make extra. Serve a crowd, or store the extras (peeled or unpeeled) in an airtight container in the fridge for up to 2 days for jazzing up all kinds of simple meals.

Cooking eggs on the stovetop isn't so hard, so what's the advantage of using the pressure cooker? First, since the timers are locked in and consistent, there's little danger of walking away and overcooking the eggs (no more fully firm yolks when you were dreaming of one that was jammy and golden). Second, peeling eggs cooked in the pressure cooker is a breeze; they slip out of their shells in near perfect form, ready to be sliced or halved.

1. Fill a large bowl with ice water and set it near the pressure cooker.

2. Fill the inner pot of the pressure cooker with about 1 cup water and place the steamer basket inside. Add the whole eggs to the steamer basket, stacking in a pyramid if needed.

3. Lock on the lid and Pressure Cook on low pressure for 5 to 8 minutes—5 minutes for soft-boiled, 8 minutes for firm but creamy yolks. (I like mine at 6 minutes, so the yolks are jammy and thick but not runny; check the egg cooking chart on page 185, for more details.)

4. Release the pressure manually and open the lid. Immediately use a slotted spoon to transfer the eggs to the ice bath. Peel the eggs once they are cool enough to handle. Serve the eggs whole or halved over toast, with a pat of butter, flaky salt, pepper, and fresh herbs, if desired.

Pumpkin Butter Yogurt Bowls

PREP TIME: 5 MINUTES
TOTAL TIME: 5 MINUTES
SERVES 4
GLUTEN-FREE VEGETARIAN

1 quart Homemade Yogurt (page 160) or store-bought plain whole-milk yogurt

1 cup From-Scratch Pumpkin Butter (page 165) or store-bought pumpkin butter

1 firm-ripe pear, cored and thinly sliced

½ cup toasted pepitas or other nuts (see page 143)

2 to 4 tablespoons creamy honey or unfiltered honey

On fall mornings when I need to throw together a quick breakfast for the family, toast with pumpkin butter is a real treat. But on days we need a protein start, I spoon out four bowls of homemade yogurt and dollop some pumpkin butter generously onto each. It's an easy breakfast that everyone is thrilled to eat. When I'm feeling more ambitious, I add thinly sliced apples or pears, toasted pepitas, and a swirl of local honey for a luxurious treat. Layer the same ingredients into jars with tight-fitting lids, for a grab-and-go breakfast you can really feel good about.

Divide the yogurt among 4 bowls; dollop each bowl with some pumpkin butter. Top with the pear slices, pepitas, and honey.

TRY THIS! RASPBERRY CHIA YOGURT CUPS
(GLUTEN-FREE VEGETARIAN)

Use this same formula to make jars of yogurt ready for quick breakfasts or to pack into school lunches. Divide 1 cup Raspberry Maple Jam (page 167) among 4 (1-cup) jars with tight-fitting lids. Add ⅓ cup plain yogurt of choice to each jar, followed by some chopped fresh pear, fresh berries, or chopped stone fruit, such as peaches. Fill each jar with another ⅓ cup yogurt and top off with a sprinkle of toasted nuts, toasted coconut (see Cook's Note, page 43), or a drizzle of honey. Seal the jars and store in the fridge for up to 3 days.

A Porridge Primer

If your experience with porridge begins and ends with oatmeal, you're in for a treat. There are so many grains out there that your warm breakfast bowl will continue to be exciting and new through all the seasons. You need add only water, salt, your milk of choice, and a good imagination (in the form of varied, exciting toppings).

Types of Grains

In this book, you'll find porridge made with rice, oats, millet, and amaranth (though you can make porridge with just about any whole grain, including cornmeal, quinoa, barley, spelt, kamut, buckwheat groats, wheat berries, or farro). I find rice, oats, millet, and amaranth make incredibly easy, likable, and consistently delicious hot cereals.

Sometimes I mix the grains—like millet with amaranth, brown rice with white rice, or oats with polenta or cornmeal—in the same pot. Many grains are even more enjoyable when they are mixed half and half; the larger and smaller grains play nicely together, helping avoid that one-note, gloopy-porridge experience some of us remember from childhood. If you have only one type of grain on hand, though, don't let that stop you—you can break up the texture of your porridge with luscious toppings (see Add Toppings, in next column).

More Salt, Less Sugar

Always add a hearty pinch or two of sea salt to the cooking water when making grains. A little salt equals a lot more flavor, and I find that I end up adding less brown sugar, maple syrup, or honey at the table.

Add Toppings

Think of all porridge as a blank canvas: it's there for you to paint on. Add a sprinkle of toasted nuts, sliced fruits, luscious jams, and a drizzle of oat milk, say, and you're well on your way to a magical morning. Use the recipes as a starting point for your own creativity. Some toppings that my family loves include: Whole Mandarin Marmalade (page 169), almond butter, honey, maple syrup, fresh figs, fresh or freeze-dried berries, bee pollen, flax seeds, toasted coconut, toasted sliced almonds, fresh persimmon, dried red currants, leftover cranberry relish. There are no wrong answers here.

All-Purpose Porridge Topper
GLUTEN-FREE, VEGETARIAN,
VEGAN, DAIRY-FREE

My favorite dreamy porridge topping is berries stewed in maple syrup until saucy. You can make this topping with fresh berries all summer long, but come fall and winter, turn to your freezer for frozen strawberries, blackberries, or mangoes. These out-of-season fruits can be quickly cooked into a juicy topping that brings porridge to life. (Here's the bonus: frozen berries release more juices and cook faster than fresh, making them a super-easy wintertime treat.) Here's how to make it:

Combine 1 pint fresh berries or 1 (12-ounce) bag frozen berries with 3 tablespoons pure maple syrup and a pinch of fine sea salt in a small pot set over medium-high heat. Cook, stirring occasionally, until the berries soften and weep, releasing their juices (you might need to add a splash of water, about 1 tablespoon, to get them started). When the berries are just soft and juicy, but not runny, stop the cooking. Let cool or serve them warm over warm porridge. Store any leftovers in a clean jar in the fridge for up to 1 week.

Coconut Rice Porridge
with Bananas, Raspberry Jam, and Coconut Chips

PREP TIME: 5 MINUTES
TOTAL TIME: 30 MINUTES
SERVES 4
GLUTEN-FREE DAIRY-FREE
VEGAN VEGETARIAN

1½ cups water

1 (13.5-ounce) can unsweetened full-fat coconut milk, plus more for drizzling

1 cup long-grain rice, such as basmati (white, brown, or a mix; see page 183)

Pinch of fine sea salt

2 ripe bananas or 1 mango, thinly sliced

2 to 4 tablespoons Raspberry Maple Jam (page 167) or store-bought jam

Toasted coconut chips (optional; see Cook's Note)

Pure maple syrup, for serving

COOK'S NOTE

Big Batch It: Toast trays of coconut chips in a 300°F degree oven until the chips are lightly toasted around the edges, 8 to 9 minutes, stirring every few minutes (watch the chips carefully—once they begin to brown, they can burn easily). Store in a sealed jar at room temperature for up to 1 month. Use the chips on top of porridges, Homemade Yogurt (page 160), or Coconut-Turmeric Rice (page 102).

For this warm, slightly sweet (and super-fast) breakfast porridge, I cook the rice in a mixture of water and coconut milk for a fragrant and comforting alternative to oatmeal. (You can find similar dishes in Southeast Asia and South America.) I love basmati rice for this, but the pressure cooker can easily work its magic on almost any long-grain rice, from white to brown. (Skip Arborio or sushi rice, which are a bit starchier; porridge tends to win more fans when it's creamy and loose.) I frequently mix brown and white rice; the white breaks down more than the brown, making for a dreamy, two-textured porridge that I adore. This is the kind of comforting breakfast that welcomes all the toppings and can easily double as dessert (served warm or cold).

1. Soak the rice in water for 15 minutes (see Cook's Note, page 102), and then rinse until the water runs clear; drain.

2. Combine 1½ cups fresh water and coconut milk in the inner pot of the pressure cooker and add the rice and salt. Lock on the lid and Pressure Cook on high pressure for 6 to 10 minutes for white rice or 20 to 22 minutes for brown rice or a mix (the longer you cook it, the creamier the porridge). Let the pressure release naturally (10 to 12 minutes), then leave the cooker on the Keep Warm setting until ready to serve.

3. Open the lid. Spoon the porridge into bowls and top with the fruit and jam, and finish with a sprinkling of coconut chips, if desired. Drizzle lightly with maple syrup and serve warm.

Millet and Amaranth Porridge
with Figs and Papaya

PREP TIME: 10 MINUTES
TOTAL TIME: 25 MINUTES
SERVES 4
GLUTEN-FREE DAIRY FREE*
VEGAN VEGETARIAN

2 cups water

⅓ cup millet, rinsed

⅓ cup amaranth, rinsed

½ to 1 teaspoon fine sea salt

½ to 1 cup cow's milk (or coconut, almond, soy, or oat milk)
*For dairy-free, use alternative milks

⅓ cup Homemade Yogurt (page 160) or store-bought plain whole-milk yogurt or kefir

2 to 4 fresh figs, sliced or halved

½ small papaya, peeled, seeded, and sliced or chopped

2 tablespoons honey

1 lime, quartered, for serving

FOR THE SLOW COOKER

Butter the interior of the slow cooker (grains and porridges tend to stick). Cook the porridge on Low for 4 hours.

Millet and amaranth are high-nutrient, texture-rich grains that cook into a creamy porridge and take on almost any flavor you want to bestow on them. Here, I mix the dense, pearl-like millet with tiny amaranth (no bigger than the tip of a pen) for a creamy, pudding-like texture that my kids love. On the stovetop, these grains require long cooking and lots of babysitting, but a pressure cooker eliminates the stirring and halves the cooking time.

This porridge is especially inviting with papaya or fresh figs—the warm and sunny flavors of the fruits do a great job of brightening up a wintry bowl of porridge. But millet and amaranth take equally well to sliced bananas, stewed fruits (see page 41), marmalades, and jams, as well as to any milk (cow's or alternative) you're craving. If you don't have fresh fruit on hand, try tossing in ½ cup raisins or chopped dried figs at the start; they'll plump up and naturally sweeten the porridge while the grains cook.

1. Add the water, millet, amaranth, and salt to the inner pot of the pressure cooker. Lock on the lid and Pressure Cook on high pressure for 12 minutes. Let the pressure release naturally (about 10 minutes), then leave the cooker on the Keep Warm setting until ready to serve.

2. Open the lid. Stir in the milk to desired consistency (I like my porridge loose but creamy). Spoon the porridge into bowls, top each serving with a dollop of yogurt, and finish with the fresh fruit and a drizzle of honey. Serve with lime wedges for squeezing over.

Steel-Cut Oat Porridge
with Peanut Butter, Chocolate, and Berries

PREP TIME: 10 MINUTES
TOTAL TIME: 20 MINUTES
SERVES 4
GLUTEN-FREE DAIRY FREE*
VEGAN VEGETARIAN

3½ cups water

1 cup steel-cut oats (or ½ cup old-fashioned rolled oats and ½ cup grits or polenta)

1 cinnamon stick

¾ teaspoon fine sea salt

½ to 1 cup unsweetened milk of choice, plus more for drizzling *For dairy-free, use alternative milks

2 tablespoons creamy peanut butter

2 to 4 ounces dark chocolate, roughly chopped

2 cups fresh berries, halved if large

2 tablespoons pure maple syrup

FOR THE SLOW COOKER

Butter the interior of the slow cooker (grains and porridges tend to stick). Cook the porridge (steel-cut oats only) using 4 cups water and cooker set on High for 4 hours or on Low for 7 hours.

In the world of hot cereals, oats reign supreme for their widespread appeal. A pressure cooker makes a great case for using steel-cut oats (also known as Irish oats). These oats otherwise take at least 30 minutes to cook but are ready in 10 minutes using a pressure cooker. If you only have, or prefer, old-fashioned (rolled) oats, mix them with heartier grains like polenta or grits, since rolled oats will turn to mush under pressure (for the same reason, don't use instant oats for this).

I cook oats in spice-infused water (with spices like fresh ginger or a cinnamon stick) and then drizzle a bit of cow's milk or almond milk, or even half-and-half, over the porridge just before serving.

1. Combine the water, oats, and cinnamon stick in the inner pot of the pressure cooker. Lock on the lid and Pressure Cook on high pressure for 10 minutes.

2. Let the pressure release naturally (10 to 12 minutes), then leave on the Keep Warm setting until ready to serve.

3. Open the lid. Stir in the milk to loosen the oats to your desired consistency, or spoon the porridge into bowls and drizzle with the milk. Top the servings with a dollop of peanut butter and some chopped chocolate and fresh berries (the peanut butter and chocolate will melt into the oats slightly). Drizzle lightly with maple syrup and serve warm.

Ricotta Toast
Three Ways

PREP TIME: 5 MINUTES
TOTAL TIME: 5 MINUTES
SERVES 4
VEGETARIAN

1 cup Creamy Homemade
   Ricotta (page 163) or
   store-bought ricotta

4 slices Perfect Toast (see box,
   page 48)

Sometimes there's no competing with simplicity. If you have read ahead to the "Staples + Mealtime Helpers" chapter and had the foresight to make batches of jam and ricotta, this can be a daily treat for breakfast or any time of day, for that matter.

1 RICOTTA AND RASPBERRY TOAST

Spoon 1 cup store bought or Creamy Homemade Ricotta (page 163) over 4 slices Perfect Toast (see box, below). Divie about ¾ cup Raspberry Maple Jam (page 167) between the toasts and serve. Feel free to swap in the Whole Mandarin Marmalade (page 169), From-Scratch Pumpkin Butter (page 165), or any jam you love atop your ricotta toast.

2 PEAR AND RICOTTA TOAST

For a decadent winter toast-topper, spoon Creamy Homemade Ricotta (page 163) over toast, then top with sliced very ripe pears or Vanilla and Cardamom Poached Pears (page 140) and a drizzle of honey.

3 SAVORY STEWED GREENS ON TOAST

For a savory take, place 4 cups trimmed and chopped hearty greens (such as chard) in the inner pot of the pressure cooker. Add ¾ cup coconut milk, 2 minced garlic cloves, ¼ teaspoon ground ginger, and ½ teaspoon fine sea salt. Lock on the lid and Pressure Cook on high pressure for 3 minutes. Release the pressure manually, then open the lid. Spoon the greens and any remaining coconut broth over the ricotta toast and sprinkle generously with freshly ground black pepper. Serve warm.

PERFECT TOAST

There's something otherworldly about a slice of sourdough bread that's been skillet-toasted in butter and olive oil (yes, both—the butter sizzles and seeps into the bread, while the oil, which can handle higher heat, helps the edges brown).

HERE'S HOW

For every 2 to 3 pieces of toast, heat 1 tablespoon each butter and extra-virgin olive oil in a large cast-iron skillet set over medium-high heat (have extra butter and oil handy for toasting the other side—how much you need depends on the bread and how buttery you like your toast). Add thick slices of sourdough, whole wheat, or baguette, and cook until toasted and golden, and the bread is starting to soak up the fat, about 3 minutes. Flip, adding another tablespoon each butter and oil, and cook until the edges are golden but the interior is still a touch soft, 2 minutes more. Serve warm.

NOURISHING
SOUPS
+ STEWS

Soups and stews are at the top of my list of soulful, easy, and endlessly inviting family meals. You can make enough for dinner tonight and extra to tuck away for tomorrow's lunch. Plus, I can get my kids to eat almost anything that is submerged in a warm, flavorful broth (with bread on the side for dunking, of course!).

An electric pressure cooker offers flexibility and ease, bringing a hearty, healthy soup or stew to the table in a fraction of the time it takes to cook in a pot on the stovetop (and even slow cookers, while slower, offer you set-it-and-forget-it ease). You *are* going to see plenty of vegetables in this chapter, and an abundance of meat and beans, too, because that's where a pressure cooker really works its brilliant magic—with ingredients that traditionally required long cooking, now shortened by pressure and steam.

Finally, the single most important part of your soup and stew game will be your garnishes—those fast, fresh, flavorful, and often deeply colorful toppings you prep while your appliance is doing all the hard work. Those herbs and other crunchy, zingy items for dolloping, stirring in, or scattering over the top are what will set your soup apart. Don't be tempted to skip them.

Soup au Pistou
with Pasta and Herbs

PREP TIME: 15 MINUTES
TOTAL TIME: 1 HOUR
5 MINUTES
SERVES 4 TO 6
VEGETARIAN

2 tablespoons extra-virgin olive oil

2 celery stalks, thinly sliced

2 medium carrots, thickly sliced

1 small yellow onion, chopped

1 bay leaf

2 garlic cloves, thinly sliced

1 teaspoon fine sea salt, plus more as needed

Freshly ground black pepper

2 medium russet potatoes, peeled and cut into ½-inch pieces

6 cups chicken or vegetable broth (such as on pages 178, 174)

1 small winter squash, peeled, seeded, and chopped, or 2 medium zucchini, cut into ½-inch pieces (about 2½ cups)

2 large Roma tomatoes, seeded and chopped, or 2 or 3 whole canned San Marzano tomatoes, drained and chopped

1 cup trimmed and chopped green beans

1 (15.5-ounce) can beans, such as cannellini, rinsed and drained

½ cup short pasta, such as medium shells, orecchiette, campanelle, or radiatore

1 cup chopped baby kale

1 cup Garlicky Pistou (see page 54), for serving

French *soupe au pistou* is one of the most vibrant soups imaginable—chock-full of vegetables. Like all my favorite soups, it benefits enormously from a flavorful stir-in—in this case the traditional pistou, a nut-free relative of Italian pesto. In a pressure cooker, you can cook the vegetables to a tender perfection in mere minutes. The beans here make the soup hearty and satisfying enough to be called dinner, though it's happily at home on the lunch table, too.

You should know that pistou welcomes just about any vegetable or bean you have. Use the ingredient list as a guide to textures and amounts, then riff to your pleasure, varying with the season. (For example, I use winter squash in the cooler months, but substitute zucchini in the summer.)

1. Pour the oil into the inner pot of the pressure cooker and set to Saute. Add the celery, carrots, onion, and bay leaf and cook, stirring frequently, until the onion is slightly softened, 8 to 10 minutes. Add the garlic, 1 teaspoon salt, and some pepper and continue cooking until fragrant, 1 minute more.

2. Add the potatoes and broth to the inner pot. Lock on the lid and Pressure Cook on high pressure for 8 minutes. Release the pressure manually and open the lid. The potatoes should be quite tender and will help thicken the broth.

3. Add the squash, tomatoes, green beans, canned beans, pasta, and kale to the pot. Lock on the lid again and Pressure Cook on high pressure for 1 to 2 minutes. Release the steam manually and open the lid. Check the pasta for doneness. If the pasta is a bit too al dente, return the lid (do not lock) and leave the soup on the Keep Warm setting for a couple of minutes.

4. Remove the bay leaf. Spoon the soup into bowls and serve warm, topped with the pistou and more salt or pepper, if desired.

(recipe continues)

GARLICKY PISTOU

PREP TIME: 5 MINUTES
TOTAL TIME: 5 MINUTES
MAKES ¾ CUP
GLUTEN-FREE VEGETARIAN

1 large bunch basil
 (about 2 packed cups)

¼ cup grated parmesan cheese
 (2 ounces)

3 garlic cloves

4 tablespoons extra-virgin
 olive oil

½ teaspoon fine sea salt

1 to 3 teaspoons hot water

The foundation of a perfect pistou is fresh basil, garlic, olive oil, salt, and grating cheese (often parmesan), the last added for body and a perfect salty-umami finish. Use whatever fine grating cheese you have on hand: parmesan, pecorino, or aged Manchego all work, as does a nutty, semi-firm cheese like Gruyère. You can make the pistou loose and shaggy, like a gremolata, but for most soups I love it blended to a creamy green paste in a food processor. Try also stirring the pistou into creamy soups, like the Celery Root Soup (page 62), in place of, or addition to, the chickpeas.

Combine the basil, cheese, garlic, olive oil, and salt in a small food processor or a blender and pulse to roughly chop. Add the hot water, 1 teaspoon at a time, to get the blade moving, and blend to make a smooth paste. You want it a touch runnier than a pesto but thick enough to easily dollop with a spoon. Refrigerate the pistou for up to 5 days in an airtight container, covered with a thin layer of olive oil to keep the basil from turning brown.

COOKING PASTA IN A PRESSURE COOKER

Cooking pasta in a pressure cooker is fast but not without its nuances. At high pressure, pasta can go from perfectly cooked to mush in mere minutes. And once the pasta is cooked through, don't leave the soup on the Keep Warm setting for longer than a few minutes because the pasta can quickly overcook. Here's a general rule of thumb: Pressure Cook the pasta for half the cooking time listed on the box, minus 2 minutes (so, 1 to 3 minutes maximum for most pastas), then drain immediately.

Chickpea Coconut Curry
with Pea Shoots

PREP TIME: 10 MINUTES
TOTAL TIME: 45 MINUTES
SERVES 4 TO 6
GLUTEN-FREE DAIRY-FREE
VEGAN* VEGETARIAN

2 tablespoons canola or
coconut oil

1 small yellow onion, finely diced

2 garlic cloves, sliced

1 teaspoon fine sea salt, plus
more if needed

1 tablespoon Madras curry
powder

Pinch of red pepper flakes

1 (14.5-ounce) can diced
tomatoes

2 (15.5-ounce) cans chickpeas,
drained

¼ head cauliflower, cut into
florets (about 2 cups)

1½ cups chicken or vegetable
broth (such as on pages 178,
174) *For vegetarian or vegan,
use vegetable broth

1 (13.5-ounce) can unsweetened
full-fat coconut milk

2 limes, half of 1 juiced, the rest
cut into wedges

Freshly ground black pepper

FOR SERVING

½ small shallot, thinly sliced

½ cup fresh cilantro or mint
leaves, or a combination

½ cup roasted cashews or
peanuts

1 small handful of fresh
pea shoots

Sometimes you need a meatless soup with the full-fat flavor and heartiness of a stew, but that's healthier and surprising in flavor. Chickpeas and coconut milk simmered into a curry really pulls off that trick here. If you're up for it, you can first cook dried chickpeas (see page 181) and then build on them, but for a decadent-feeling weeknight fix, canned chickpeas work beautifully.

1. Pour the oil into the inner pot of the pressure cooker and set to Saute. Add the onion and cook, stirring often, until slightly softened, 5 to 6 minutes. Add the garlic and salt; continue to cook until fragrant, another 1 to 2 minutes. Add the curry powder and red pepper flakes and cook, stirring rapidly, to toast the spices (but not burn them), about 30 seconds more.

2. Add the tomatoes, chickpeas, cauliflower, and broth to the pot. Lock on the lid and Pressure Cook on high pressure for 5 minutes. Release the pressure naturally.

3. Open the lid and stir in the coconut milk, then cover with the lid again and hold on the Keep Warm setting until ready to serve.

4. Just before serving, open the lid. Use an immersion blender to blend about half the chickpeas, or mash them with a potato masher (or transfer some of the soup to an upright blender and puree, then return it to the pot). Stir in the lime juice. Taste and adjust the salt and pepper, if necessary.

5. Spoon the soup into bowls and serve warm, topped with shallot, cilantro, cashews, and pea shoots (if using). Garnish with the lime wedges.

TRY THIS! CREAMY COCONUT-CHICKPEA SOUP

If you prefer a creamier soup, skip the cauliflower and puree the finished soup completely before garnishing.

Super-Quick Broccoli-Pea Soup

PREP TIME: 5 MINUTES
TOTAL TIME: 30 MINUTES
SERVES 4
GLUTEN-FREE* DAIRY-FREE*
VEGAN* VEGETARIAN

3½ cups chicken or vegetable broth (such as on pages 178, 174)

1 medium head of broccoli, cut into florets (about 4 cups) or 4 cups frozen florets (see Cook's Note)

8 ounces fresh shelled or frozen peas (see Cook's Note)

1 small head of fennel, trimmed and quartered

¾ teaspoon fine sea salt

Freshly ground black pepper

FOR SERVING

¾ cup freshly grated parmesan cheese or Homemade Yogurt (page 160) or Cashew Cream (see variation, page 151) *For dairy-free or vegan, use cashew cream

Extra-virgin olive oil

Flaky sea salt, such as Maldon

Crispy Bread Croutons, optional (see page 58) *For gluten-free, omit croutons

Sometimes you need a weeknight soup that is quick as a wink to cook, with vibrant flavor and color—something you can repeat often and still win raves from your crowd, with just tiny tweaks to keep it fresh and surprising. I often make this topped with a creamy dollop of yogurt or homemade vegan cashew cream, or a generous dusting of parmesan (think: a healthier cheesy-broccoli soup moment!). When it comes to the core ingredients, there's loads of flexibility here, too. If I'm out of peas, I can increase the broccoli (or vice versa) or swap in celery for the fennel.

1. Combine the broth, broccoli, peas, and fennel in the inner pot of the pressure cooker. Lock on the lid and Pressure Cook on high pressure for 2 minutes. Release the steam manually.

2. Open the lid and remove the inner pot from the cooker. Use an immersion blender to puree the soup until smooth (or transfer to an upright blender and puree in batches), about 3 minutes. Season with fine sea salt and some pepper. Return the inner pot to the pressure cooker with the lid off (to maintain the bright green color) and leave on the Keep Warm setting until you are ready to serve.

3. Spoon the soup into bowls and serve warm, topped with the parmesan, yogurt, or cashew cream. Drizzle with some olive oil and finish with a sprinkle of flaky salt and more pepper, if desired. Serve with croutons, if you like.

COOK'S NOTE

For the Love of Frozen: For the broccoli and peas here, note that either fresh or frozen will work, making this another great all-weather standby. Frozen vegetables not only save a bit of prep time, but they also keep the color a bright, punchy green.

COOK'S NOTE

Flashy Finish: For a hearty, eye-popping finish, top this soup with Fennel-Roasted Chickpeas (page 64) or Shaggy Parmesan Gremolata (see box, page 75).

CRISPY BREAD CROUTONS
VEGETARIAN

Good homemade croutons are a downright game changer for soups and salads. I don't put them in every batch of soup, but certain soups, like Super-Quick Broccoli-Pea Soup (page 57) and Creamy Carrot Soup (page 65), become instant favorites when topped with crunchy toasted bread. Use the best bread you can—like a sourdough miche, a good French baguette, or an Italian ciabatta—and skip the pre-sliced bread; you want to be able to cut the bread yourself so as to have substantial cubes. While your soup cooks to perfection in the pressure cooker, use your free hands to cut and toast the cubes in a skillet with butter and olive oil. (Yes, both! The butter sizzles and seeps into the bread, while the oil, which can handle the higher heat, helps brown the edges. I use the same technique for Perfect Toast; see box, page 48.)

For 4 cups of croutons (6 to 8 servings), cut 4 to 6 thick slices of bread into ½- to ¾-inch cubes (crusts left on or shaved off—your preference). Heat 1 tablespoon each butter and extra-virgin olive oil in a large cast-iron skillet set over medium-high heat. Add the cubed bread in batches, and toast, tossing frequently, until golden on all sides, 3 to 4 minutes. Transfer to a plate and season with fine sea salt or flaky Maldon salt, and set aside to cool completely.

Store the croutons at room temperature in a plastic bag or airtight container for up to 3 days. Don't be tempted to wrap them up while they're still even a tiny bit warm, or they'll steam and turn stale. It's the crunch you're after, and the only way to preserve that is to store the croutons completely cooled.

RYE, WALNUT, OR OLIVE BREAD CROUTONS
For variation, use your favorite artisan bread. Mine are seeded rye bread, olive ciabatta, or walnut loaf for big flavor and good crunch.

CRISPY TOFU CROUTONS
GLUTEN-FREE (USE GLUTEN-FREE
FLOUR FOR DUSTING) DAIRY-FREE
VEGAN VEGETARIAN

These crispy cubes are not only delicious slathered in soy sauce and served over rice, but they're also excellent swimming in soup or scattered atop a salad or grain bowl, providing a vegetarian protein or serving as a gluten-free crouton. Try them in Creamy Carrot Soup (page 65) or in place of the plain tofu in Kimchi and Tofu Stew (page 78).

Drain 1 (12-ounce) block of firm or extra-firm tofu in a colander with a plate set on top, for 20 minutes. Cut into ½- to 1-inch pieces, then lay the pieces out on a paper towel-lined plate to drain further, patting dry on all sides.

Heat a large nonstick or cast-iron skillet over medium-high heat. Add ⅓ to ½ cup neutral oil (such as canola) and heat until shimmering. Lightly dust the tofu cubes with all-purpose flour or a gluten-free flour blend, tapping off the excess. Carefully (it will splatter) add the tofu cubes to the skillet and cook until golden on all sides, about 4 minutes per side. Season well with salt, pepper, and any other seasonings that you love, and use within a day.

Spring White Bean Soup
with Fresh Herbs

(a.k.a. DETOX SOUP)

PREP TIME: 10 MINUTES
TOTAL TIME: 30 MINUTES
SERVES 6
GLUTEN-FREE* DAIRY-FREE
VEGAN* VEGETARIAN*

1 pound dried large white beans, such as Corona or Gigante, soaked overnight and drained

8 cups chicken or vegetable broth (such as on pages 178, 174) *For vegan and vegetarian, use vegetable broth

1 small yellow onion, halved

3 celery stalks, halved

8 parsley stems (leaves reserved for garnish)

4 garlic cloves, thinly sliced

1 tablespoon fine sea salt, plus more as needed

Freshly ground black pepper

3 to 4 cups prepped fresh spring vegetables, such as thinly sliced asparagus, shelled peas, halved haricots verts or green beans, torn leafy greens, or a combination

FOR SERVING

½ cup extra-virgin olive oil

1 packed cup mixed herbs (dill, mint, and/or parsley), torn or roughly chopped

½ cup pomegranate seeds

1 lemon, cut into wedges

Sometimes you're looking for a soup that is healthful and clean but still satisfying, a soup that leaves you feeling as if you've just eaten a big, vibrant salad (but without the desire to eat a whole plate of fries afterward). For me, this bean soup fits the bill. I hope it does for you, too.

If you crave big flavors, don't skimp on the garnish. Shaggy herbs and bright pomegranate seeds give the soup a surprise finish and a bright pop of color without demanding a lot of extra work.

Feel free to play around with the in-season vegetables here. This could have asparagus or, if you have the time, trimmed artichokes.

1. Combine the beans, broth, onion, celery, parsley stems, garlic, 1 tablespoon salt, and some pepper in the inner pot of the pressure cooker. Lock on the lid and Pressure Cook on high pressure for 20 minutes. Release the pressure manually. Open the lid and check; the beans should be tender and creamy.

2. With tongs, remove and discard the onion, celery, and parsley stems.

3. Add the spring vegetables to the inner pot. Lock on the lid again and Pressure Cook for 0 minutes on high pressure (yes, 0 minutes— the vegetables will cook in the time it takes the pressure cooker to build pressure, while staying bright green). Release the steam manually and open the lid.

4. Stir together the olive oil and herbs in a small bowl. Spoon the soup into bowls, top with the herb mixture, and sprinkle on the pomegranate seeds. Serve with lemon wedges and toast, if desired.

Celery Root Soup
with Radish, Fennel-Roasted Chickpeas, and Parsley

PREP TIME: 5 MINUTES
TOTAL TIME: 45 MINUTES
SERVES 4
GLUTEN-FREE VEGETARIAN

1 large or 2 small celery roots (about 2 pounds total), peeled and quartered

4 cups chicken or vegetable broth (such as on pages 178, 174)

1 teaspoon fine sea salt, or more to taste

1 to 1½ cups heavy cream or half-and-half

1 tablespoon unsalted butter, or more to taste

FOR SERVING

1 large radish or 4 small radishes, thinly sliced

⅓ cup roughly chopped fresh parsley, dill, rosemary, or a combination

Extra-virgin olive oil

Flaky sea salt, such as Maldon

Freshly ground black pepper

Fennel-Roasted Chickpeas, optional (see page 64)

This creamy all-weather soup wins fans for its clean flavor and big, bold finish—with snappy radishes and chickpeas. This is a pared-down (read: fast!) soup with virtually no prep time—that said, please don't skip making the vibrant herb-and-radish garnish, which really boosts the finish, flavor-wise (use any radishes you have and love, from small Easter Egg or breakfast radishes to bold watermelon radishes). If you're a squash soup fan, you can swap the celery root for butternut (or kabocha) squash. For an extra crouton-like finish, try the Fennel-Roasted Chickpeas (see page 64)—an optional, but delicious, final touch.

1. Combine the celery root, broth, and 1 teaspoon salt in the inner pot of the pressure cooker. Lock on the lid and Pressure Cook on high pressure for 20 to 25 minutes; the more you cook it, the creamier the soup. Let the pressure release naturally (15 minutes), then release the remaining pressure manually and leave on the Keep Warm setting.

2. Meanwhile, prepare the Fennel-Roasted Chickpeas, if using.

3. Open the lid and puree the soup with an immersion blender (or in an upright blender) until completely smooth and creamy, adding the cream, butter, and salt to taste (remember that you will get a *lot* of flavor from the garnish at the end). Add a little less cream if you like a clean celery-root flavor or more cream if you're looking for something rich and decadent. Stir, then leave on the Keep Warm setting until the mixture is warmed through.

4. Spoon the soup into bowls and serve warm, topped with the radish and herbs. Drizzle lightly with the olive oil and sprinkle with the flaky salt and more pepper, if desired. Serve sprinkled with the chickpeas, if using.

(recipe continues on page 64)

FENNEL-ROASTED CHICKPEAS

PREP TIME: 5 MINUTES
TOTAL TIME: 15 MINUTES
MAKES 1½ CUPS
GLUTEN-FREE DAIRY-FREE
VEGAN VEGETARIAN

1 (15.5-ounce) can chickpeas,
    drained

2 tablespoons extra-virgin
    olive oil

1 teaspoon fennel seeds

Flaky sea salt, such as Maldon

Freshly ground black pepper

This quick, savory stovetop treat is incredible atop creamy vegetable soups and raw salads as a gluten-free crouton stand-in (and protein booster). The chickpeas also make an incredible snack on their own, so feel free to double the recipe and keep them at the ready.

Turn the chickpeas out onto a paper towel–lined sheet pan and pat them dry with paper towels to remove excess moisture; set aside for about 10 minutes to dry out.

Heat the olive oil in a large cast-iron skillet over high heat until shimmering (a chickpea should sizzle when added). Add the chickpeas and fennel seeds and cook, tossing occasionally, until the chickpeas are crispy and lightly browned, 5 to 8 minutes. Season generously with flaky salt and pepper. Keep warm in the pan for immediately topping a soup, or cool and store in an airtight container for up to 3 days.

Creamy Carrot Soup

PREP TIME: 8 MINUTES
TOTAL TIME: 40 MINUTES
SERVES 4 TO 6
GLUTEN-FREE* DAIRY-FREE
VEGAN* VEGETARIAN*

2 pounds carrots, scrubbed and trimmed

4½ to 5 cups chicken or vegetable broth (such as on pages 178, 174)
*For vegan and vegetarian, use vegetable broth

2 tablespoons extra-virgin olive oil, plus more for serving

1 garlic clove, smashed

1 (1-inch) piece peeled fresh ginger, sliced into coins

1 teaspoon fine sea salt, plus more as needed

Freshly ground black pepper

1 to 2 tablespoons white miso paste

FOR SERVING

1 lemon, halved

3 to 4 tablespoons chopped or snipped fresh chives

Crispy Bread Croutons (see page 58) or Crispy Tofu Croutons (see page 59)
*For gluten-free, use gluten-free bread for croutons or omit

COOK'S NOTE

About Miso: Miso is a fermented soybean paste used in Japanese cooking that adds depth and salty umami to many foods. Since it lasts virtually forever (literally years in the fridge), I keep it on hand for whisking into broths and other soups like this one or for making quick miso soups. It comes in many colors, but white miso (which is actually an amber yellow color) is a good choice for this recipe.

Carrot soup is a reliable, please-all soup worth returning to again and again. For many years I preferred my carrot soup with a clean, sweet finish, thanks to a splash of fresh carrot juice at the end. These days, with the ease of a pressure cooker, I can add all my ingredients to the pot at once, getting a similar bright flavor from whole peeled carrots. The addition of miso paste here supplies the umami and works as a seasoning, but it isn't required. Do add the chives and croutons, if you're in the mood.

1. Combine the carrots, broth, olive oil, garlic, ginger, and 1 teaspoon salt in the inner pot of the pressure cooker. Lock on the lid and Pressure Cook on high pressure for 8 minutes. Release the steam manually, then open the lid. Check to ensure the ginger and carrots are completely tender; if not, lock on the lid again and Pressure Cook on high pressure for 2 minutes more.

2. Open the lid. Use an immersion blender to puree the soup until smooth, about 3 minutes (or blend in batches in an upright blender). Add the miso (if using) and season with salt and pepper as needed—if you skip the miso, you may need up to ½ teaspoon more salt. Blend until creamy and smooth, another 2 to 3 minutes. Taste and adjust the seasoning, if needed.

3. Return the inner pot to the pressure cooker and leave on the Keep Warm setting until you are ready to serve.

4. Spoon the soup into bowls, squeeze the lemon over the top, and serve warm, topped with chives and croutons, if desired.

TRY THIS! CREAM OF CARROT SOUP
(GLUTEN-FREE VEGETARIAN)

For a creamier carrot soup, stir ½ to 1 cup heavy cream or coconut milk into the pureed soup and warm it thoroughly before serving.

Red Lentil Dal
with Citrus and Herbs

PREP TIME: 15 MINUTES
TOTAL TIME: 30 MINUTES
SERVES 4
GLUTEN-FREE DAIRY-FREE*
VEGAN AND VEGETARIAN

1 cup masoor dal (split red lentils)

5 to 6 cups vegetable broth (such as on page 174) or water

1 large red onion, finely chopped (about 1½ cups)

2 large ripe tomatoes (about 1 pound), cored and chopped

2 to 3 green chiles, such as serrano or jalapeño, halved

1 tablespoon finely grated peeled fresh ginger

¼ teaspoon ground turmeric

2 teaspoons ground coriander

1 teaspoon ground cumin

1 tablespoon lemon juice

Fine sea salt

FOR SERVING

3 garlic cloves, thinly sliced

4 tablespoons ghee (clarified butter; see Cook's Note) or coconut oil, melted *For dairy-free. use coconut oil

1 cup fresh cilantro leaves

¼ cup fresh mint leaves

1 lemon or lime, thinly sliced

I fell in love with dal—an Indian lentil-based soup—after marrying a vegetarian. Red lentils make for a quicker, easier, and—for me—way more satisfying plant-based protein fix than green or brown lentils, which take longer to cook and can be hard to digest. Red lentils, which are brown lentils minus the hulls, break down quickly and offer a blank slate for other flavors. It is a common soup in an Indian kitchen, infused with the spices of the *masala dabba* (a spice box used for keeping day-to-day spices which varies from region to region, and home to home). This base of brothy red lentils is really just the beginning: as with the Breakfast Congee (page 36), it's the myriad toppings that really carry the dish. I love this with loads of lemon and cilantro, a little hint of mint, and crispy garlic chips—though just a sprinkle of cilantro and a squeeze of lemon can sometimes be just right (see the variation that follows). And with a pressure cooker, you can have it all in 30 minutes flat.

1. Combine the dal, 5 cups of the broth, the red onion, tomatoes, chiles, ginger, turmeric, coriander, and cumin in the inner pot of the pressure cooker. Lock on the lid and Pressure Cook on high pressure for 15 minutes. Release the steam naturally (about 15 minutes). Open the lid and check; the lentils should be falling apart.

2. Meanwhile, in a medium cast-iron skillet over medium heat, cook the garlic in the ghee until crisp and golden, stirring frequently and adjusting the heat to avoid burning, about 2 minutes. Use a slotted spoon to transfer the garlic to a paper towel to drain.

3. Taste the dal and adjust the consistency with the remaining 1 cup broth if you like. Stir in the lemon juice; add salt if needed.

4. Spoon the dal into bowls and top with the garlic chips and the cilantro, mint, and lemon slices.

TRY THIS! SPICY SAMBAL LENTILS

If you're in a rush and don't have time for making the crispy garlic chips, but you still want a warming fix with a little kick, stir in some sambal oelek—an Indonesian chile paste made of crushed red chiles, vinegar, and salt—and finish with cilantro, mint and lemon.

COOK'S NOTE

Better Than Butter: Ghee, a nutty-tasting clarified butter traditionally used in Indian cooking, is my favorite fat for toasting spices, giving a warming aroma to many savory meals. It's even ideal for popping popcorn! Ghee has a buttery finish and a high smoke point (unlike regular butter), meaning it won't burn in the time it takes your onions to brown or your kernels to pop. Flavored ghees, like garlic-flavored ghee, lend a lovely aroma without any extra work.

Turkey Meatball Soup
with Macaroni and Kale

PREP TIME: 15 MINUTES
TOTAL TIME: 1 HOUR
SERVES 6

1 pound lean ground turkey, pork, or a combination

¼ cup panko bread crumbs

⅓ packed cup finely chopped fresh parsley leaves

1 teaspoon dried thyme or oregano

1 large egg, lightly beaten

3 garlic cloves, minced

1 teaspoon fine sea salt, plus more as needed

½ teaspoon black pepper, plus more as needed

½ cup finely grated pecorino or parmesan cheese, plus more for serving

2 tablespoons extra-virgin olive oil, plus more for drizzling

8 cups chicken broth (such as on page 178)

1 cup macaroni

4 packed cups chopped baby kale

1 lemon, zested and cut in half

⅓ packed cup roughly chopped fresh dill or basil, for serving

My kids love Italian Wedding soup—small meatballs and pasta floating in a fragrant chicken broth—more than almost any other soup. I've been making them this recipe for years and even published a version of it in the *New York Times*.

When an electric pressure cooker came into my life, I was skeptical about trying our go-to soup in it: Would the meatballs fall apart into a million pieces under pressure? But (in the name of research), I gave it a go. The result: the meatballs were exceptionally moist and tender, and they lent the broth a deeply flavorful finish—a big reward for the little trouble they caused. Plus, there was only one pot to clean, which always wins, in my book.

This is one of the fussier recipes in the book, simply because browning the meatballs in an electric pressure cooker is not *the easiest*. But the reward is there. You *can*, alternatively, brown the meatballs in a skillet before you begin—either way, don't skip this family favorite (and try these tender meatballs in the Quick Pomodoro Sauce on page 173, too!).

1. Combine the meat, bread crumbs, parsley, thyme, egg, garlic, 1 teaspoon salt, ½ teaspoon pepper, and the cheese in a large bowl. Mix with a fork or clean hands until well combined. Gently roll the mixture into 16 medium (1¾-inch) or about 32 small (1-inch) meatballs.

2. Pour 1 tablespoon of the oil into the inner pot of the pressure cooker and set to Saute. Add half the meatballs and brown on all sides, turning them carefully, about 2 minutes per side. Transfer the browned meatballs to a plate and repeat with the remaining tablespoon oil and the remaining meatballs.

3. Once the second batch is browned, return the first batch of meatballs to the inner pot, and add the broth and macaroni. Lock on the lid and Pressure Cook on high pressure for 2 minutes. Release the steam manually (covering your pressure valve with a

(recipe continues)

These meatballs are dynamite when pressure cooked in 4 cups Quick Pomodoro Sauce (page 173) on high pressure for 4 minutes (no need to brown them first, though you can if you'd like!). Roll the meatballs slightly larger, making 12 large (2-inch) or 16 medium (1¼-inch) meatballs, and butter the inner pot of the pressure cooker before adding the sauce (so the meatballs don't stick). After cooking, release the pressure manually and open the lid. Serve over spaghetti or stuff into hoagie rolls for a juicy meatball sandwich (serves 4).

towel, as it may sputter, thanks to the starch in the pasta). Open the lid. Check the pasta for doneness; also check a meatball to be sure it is cooked through. If needed, put on the lid again (but don't lock) and let sit on the Keep Warm setting for 2 minutes more.

4. Open the lid and add the kale and lemon zest to the pot. Stir once, replace the lid (but don't lock), and leave on the Keep Warm setting until the greens are wilted, 1 to 3 minutes, opening the lid and stirring occasionally if needed. Season with additional salt and pepper to taste.

5. Open the lid and spoon the soup into bowls. Drizzle with a little olive oil and lemon juice. Scatter the cheese and herbs over the top.

Green Pozole
(with All the Fixings)

PREP TIME: 15 MINUTES
TOTAL TIME: 40 MINUTES
SERVES 6 TO 8
GLUTEN-FREE

1 tablespoon extra-virgin olive oil

1 medium white onion, roughly chopped

3 poblano chiles, seeded and coarsely chopped

1 teaspoon fine sea salt, plus more as needed

1 pound tomatillos, husked, rinsed, and quartered

6 cups chicken or vegetable broth (such as on pages 178, 174)

1 bunch fresh cilantro leaves and fine stems, roughly chopped

1 pound skinless, boneless chicken breast, cut into ½-inch pieces

1 (28-ounce) can white hominy, drained

Freshly ground black pepper

2 limes, halved

FOR SERVING

4 radishes, thinly sliced

1 firm-ripe avocado, peeled and chopped

1 green chile, thinly sliced

Fresh cilantro leaves, torn

Cotija cheese or queso fresco, crumbled

⅓ cup toasted pumpkin seeds or tortilla chips

1 lime, cut into wedges

Pozole is a filling traditional Mexican soup made with hominy and chicken, pork, or other stew meats, depending on the region. It's the kind of soup I crave often but make only once in a blue moon, owing to its many steps. A pressure cooker, though, offers a genius shortcut, allowing the base of green tomatillos to be made right in the pot (as opposed to under a broiler or in a separate pan) and the chicken to be poached right in the broth. It's tangy yet soothing and easy to tailor the toppings to each person's preference (red onions for my husband, lime and radishes for me, and avocado and cheese for the kids).

1. Pour the oil into the inner pot of the pressure cooker and set to Saute. Add the onion, chiles, and 1 teaspoon salt and cook until the onion softens, about 8 minutes. Add the tomatillos and broth, lock on the lid, and Pressure Cook on high pressure for 10 minutes. Release the steam manually and open the lid. The vegetables should be completely tender.

2. Let cool slightly, then add the cilantro (the herb will turn brown if you add it too early). Puree the soup with an immersion blender (or cool slightly and process in batches in an upright blender).

3. Stir in the chicken and hominy. Lock on the lid again and Pressure Cook on high pressure for 4 minutes. Release the pressure manually and open the lid. The chicken should be just cooked through but tender.

4. Taste and add salt and pepper, if needed. Squeeze in the lime halves, and stir. Spoon the soup into bowls and garnish with the radishes, avocado, chile, cilantro, and cheese. Top with the toasted pumpkin seeds or serve with tortilla chips. Serve warm with the lime wedges.

FOR THE SLOW COOKER

Make the pozole up to step 1 in the slow cooker. Cook on High for 3 hours. Add the cilantro and puree the mixture, then return it to the slow cooker along with the chicken and hominy and cook 1 hour more on High.

Traditional Beef Borscht

PREP TIME: 20 MINUTES
TOTAL TIME: 1 HOUR 30 MINUTES
SERVES 4 TO 6
GLUTEN-FREE DAIRY-FREE*

1 tablespoon extra-virgin olive oil

2 medium carrots, thickly sliced

1 small onion, thinly sliced

1 celery stalk, sliced

1 bay leaf

1 garlic clove, thinly sliced

1½ pounds bone-in beef short ribs or ½ rack pork ribs, such as baby back

6 cups beef or chicken broth (such as on pages 176, 178), or water

1 teaspoon fine sea salt, plus more as needed

2 medium beets, peeled and cut into 1-inch pieces

5 small white or red potatoes, scrubbed and cut in half

3 tablespoons tomato paste

¼ small head of green cabbage, cored and cut into 1-inch pieces

1 teaspoon distilled white vinegar

Freshly ground black pepper

FOR SERVING

Sour cream or Homemade Yogurt (page 160), optional
  *For dairy-free, omit sour cream

Handful of fresh dill, roughly chopped

COOK'S NOTE

Beets to Go: Many general grocery stores now carry peeled cooked beets in their produce sections—the beets are usually vacuum sealed in plastic packages. If you're short on time, feel free to use such cooked beets instead, adding them along with the cabbage at the end (but note that the color or beet flavor won't be as vibrant).

There's a famous Russian cafe in New York City called Petrossian, which serves the most excellent borscht; I love eating a bowlful of that potent, flavorful soup. But borscht, usually made with beef broth and beets, can be such a chore to make at home. Enter the electric pressure cooker, with which you can create this healthful classic in one fell swoop. Yes, there are still a few steps here, but the work is cut in half. If you prefer, you can make a vegetarian version (skip the beef and use vegetable broth in place of the water), but the beef bones really do add a nourishing oomph—especially welcome if you live someplace where winters are cold and long.

1. Pour the oil into the inner pot of the pressure cooker and set to Saute. Add the carrots, onion, celery, and bay leaf and cook, stirring frequently, until the onion softens slightly, about 5 minutes. Add the garlic and continue cooking until fragrant, 1 to 2 minutes more.

2. Add the short ribs, broth, and 1 teaspoon salt to the pot. Lock on the lid and Pressure Cook on high pressure for 25 minutes. Manually release the pressure, open the lid, and transfer the short ribs to a plate. Skim the broth of excess fat. Remove the bay leaf.

3. Pull the meat off the bones and roughly chop (discard the bones or save them for a future broth). Return the meat to the inner pot along with the beets, potatoes, and tomato paste and stir. Lock on the lid again and Pressure Cook on high pressure for 4 minutes. Manually release the pressure and open the lid.

4. Add the cabbage to the pot, put on the lid again (but don't lock), and leave on the Keep Warm setting for at least 3 minutes, or until ready to serve.

5. Just before serving, open the lid and stir in the vinegar. Adjust the salt and pepper, if needed. Spoon the soup into bowls and serve warm, topped with sour cream and dill.

Bacon, Salmon, and Corn Chowder

PREP TIME: 20 MINUTES
TOTAL TIME: 1 HOUR 15 MINUTES
SERVES 4 TO 6
GLUTEN-FREE

1 tablespoon unsalted butter

8 ounces bacon, roughly chopped

1 small onion or 1 large shallot (or 4 scallions, white parts only), minced

3 celery stalks, finely chopped

3 garlic cloves, finely chopped

2 large russet potatoes, peeled and cut into 1-inch pieces

4 cups chicken or vegetable broth (such as on pages 178, 174)

1½ teaspoons fine sea salt, plus more as needed

½ teaspoon freshly ground black pepper, plus more as needed

1½ pounds wild or sockeye salmon fillet, skin discarded and pin bones removed, cut into 1-inch pieces

2 cups fresh or frozen corn kernels

2 cups half-and-half

FOR SERVING

1 bunch chives, snipped; or 2 scallions, green part thinly sliced

1 green chile, such as jalapeño, thinly sliced

A good Nordic fish chowder is a lighter relative of America's New England clam chowder, made here with wild or sockeye salmon instead of clams. In the pressure cooker, it comes together almost instantly, with the tender potatoes, at once both filling and soothing, ready to take on the flavors of whatever you throw at them. For the base recipe here, I use bacon, potatoes, and corn; I add green chiles for heat; and top with tons of herbs for a fresh finish. Vegetarians can omit the salmon and make the variation that follows, either eliminating the bacon or swapping in plant-based bacon.

1. Add the butter to the inner pot of the pressure cooker and set to Saute. When the butter melts, add the bacon and cook, stirring often, until beginning to crisp, 8 to 10 minutes. Remove the bacon and drain on paper towels.

2. Add the onion to the bacon fat and cook, stirring, until slightly softened, about 4 minutes. Add the celery and garlic and continue cooking until fragrant, 2 minutes more.

3. Add the potatoes, broth, salt, and pepper to the inner pot. Lock on the lid and Pressure Cook on high pressure for 3 to 4 minutes. Release the pressure manually.

4. Open the lid and stir in the salmon and corn. Lock on the lid again and leave on the Keep Warm setting until the corn is tender and the salmon is cooked through, about 3 minutes.

5. Open the lid and stir in the half-and-half. Loosely cover and leave on the Keep Warm setting until heated through, about 2 minutes.

6. Taste and adjust the seasoning with salt and pepper, as desired. Spoon the soup into bowls and top with chives, chile, and crispy bacon.

TRY THIS! POTATO AND CORN CHOWDER

For a potato take on this easy favorite, skip the salmon and serve the chowder with ⅓ cup shredded Cheddar sprinkled onto each steaming bowl.

Brothy Beef Stew with Dill

PREP TIME: 15 MINUTES
TOTAL TIME: 1 HOUR 45 MINUTES
SERVES 6 TO 8
GLUTEN-FREE DAIRY-FREE

2 tablespoons extra-virgin olive oil

1½ pounds boneless beef stew meat, such as chuck, cut into 1½-inch pieces

1 large yellow onion, thinly sliced

3 celery stalks, cut into ½-inch pieces

2 garlic cloves, thinly sliced

6 cups beef or chicken broth (such as on pages 176, 178)

5 large carrots, cut into ½-inch pieces

1 bay leaf

1 teaspoon fine sea salt, plus more as needed

Freshly ground black pepper

3 medium red or white potatoes, cut into 2-inch pieces

6 whole canned San Marzano tomatoes, coarsely chopped

¼ small head of green cabbage, cored and cut into ½-inch pieces

1 cup fresh dill, torn or chopped, for serving

My favorite beef stews are more soup than stew—neither thick or gloopy but, rather, brothy and clean-tasting, with just enough beef to flavor the broth deeply without overpowering the unsung heroes, the big chunks of vegetables I want to see on my spoon as I lap up all the flavor. I could eat this weekly as a fortifying lunch or dinner, but when I want to dress it up—for company or on the weekend—the Shaggy Parmesan Gremolata (see box below) does the trick. And I can't imagine this without a lavishly buttered roll, for dunking.

1. Pour the olive oil into the inner pot of the pressure cooker and set to Saute. Add the stew meat and cook until the meat is beginning to brown on all sides, about 8 minutes. Add the onion and celery and cook, stirring occasionally, until the onion is slightly softened, about 8 minutes more. Add the garlic and continue cooking until the garlic is fragrant, 1 minute more.

2. Add the broth, carrots, bay leaf, and 1 teaspoon salt and pepper, to taste, to the inner pot, stirring a few times with a wooden spoon to scrape the meat bits off the bottom of the pan. Lock on the lid and Pressure Cook on high pressure for 20 minutes. Release the pressure manually and open the lid.

3. Add the potatoes, tomatoes, and cabbage. Lock on the lid again and Pressure Cook on high pressure for 3 to 4 minutes. Release the steam manually and leave on the Keep Warm setting until ready to serve.

4. Open the lid. Taste and adjust the salt and pepper as needed. Spoon the soup into bowls and serve warm, topped with the dill.

SHAGGY PARMESAN GREMOLATA
(GLUTEN-FREE, VEGETARIAN)

Beef stew does just fine topped with heaps of dill, but a little extra zing from a classic gremolata (a garlicky, lemon- and herb-flecked sprinkle–in this case, laced with parmesan) really gets the party started. Use this to top any of the soups in this chapter.

TO MAKE IT: Combine ¼ cup finely chopped fresh parsley, 2 tablespoons finely grated lemon zest (preferably on a microplane), 2 minced or grated garlic cloves, 2 tablespoons chopped or torn fresh dill, 1 tablespoon chopped or torn fresh mint, and 2 tablespoons finely grated parmesan in a bowl. Refrigerate for up to 1 day. (Makes about 1 cup)

FOR THE SLOW COOKER

In a pan on the stovetop, cook the onion and celery in the oil until tender, about 3 minutes. Add the stew meat and garlic, and cook until browned, about 5 minutes. Transfer to the slow cooker, along with 5 cups of broth (instead of 6), the carrots, bay leaf, 1 teaspoon salt, the potatoes, tomatoes, and carrots. Cook on Low for 8 to 10 hours. Season with salt and pepper to taste.

Holiday Ham and Navy Bean Soup
with Rosemary and Escarole

PREP TIME: 20 MINUTES
TOTAL TIME: 2 HOURS
30 MINUTES
SERVES 6
GLUTEN-FREE DAIRY-FREE

1 tablespoon extra-virgin olive oil

1 large onion, halved and sliced (about 2 cups)

2 celery stalks, cut into 1-inch pieces (about 1 cup)

2 medium carrots, scrubbed and cut into 1-inch pieces (about 1 cup)

2 bay leaves

1 large sprig fresh rosemary

1½ pounds leftover ham bone (with meat remaining) or osso bucco or bone-in ham shank

10 cups pork broth (such as on page 177) or water

1 teaspoon pure maple syrup

1 teaspoon fine sea salt, plus more to taste

½ teaspoon freshly ground black pepper, plus more as needed

1½ cups dried navy beans (or bean soup mix), rinsed

4 packed cups chopped escarole or other sturdy greens, like mustard greens or kale

¾ cup roughly chopped fresh parsley, dill, or a combination, for garnish

This soup channels a classic ham dinner, rich with bay leaf and rosemary flavors, and even a touch of maple syrup, without the 3-hour cook time. It's a great soup to make the day after a baked ham dinner—why waste all that good meat and flavor clinging to the bone? But don't wait for the holidays; this is deeply satisfying when made with osso bucco or a ham shank, any time of the year.

Here, the flavor is the very best when the ham bones sit in the pot of beans in the fridge overnight, enabling the beans to soak up even more flavor; so, if you can plan ahead, make this soup the day before you intend to serve it.

1. Pour the olive oil into the inner pot of the pressure cooker and set to Saute. Add the onion, celery, carrots, bay leaves, and rosemary and cook, stirring occasionally, until the onion is slightly softened, about 8 minutes.

2. Add the ham bone, broth, maple syrup, 1 teaspoon salt, ½ teaspoon pepper, and the beans. Lock on the lid and Pressure Cook on high pressure for 35 minutes. Let the pressure release naturally (about 45 minutes), then open the lid.

3. Transfer the ham bone to a plate; pull the meat off the bone and discard the bone. Return the meat to the inner pot. Skim any excess fat from the soup and discard the bay leaves and rosemary stem. Stir in the escarole while the soup is on the Keep Warm setting and allow it to wilt.

4. Spoon the soup into bowls and garnish with herbs. Add more salt or pepper to taste, if desired.

FOR THE SLOW COOKER

Prepare the soup up to step 2 in the slow cooker. Cook on High for 6 hours or on Low for 10 hours, then proceed to step 3.

COOK'S NOTE

Fresh Bean Alternative: If you can get your hands on them, fresh shelling beans, like cranberry beans, work brilliantly here. Just be sure to cut the cooking time in half. If you want to use canned beans, stir them in at the end, along with the greens.

Kimchi and Tofu Stew

PREP TIME: 15 MINUTES
TOTAL TIME: 40 MINUTES
SERVES 6
GLUTEN-FREE DAIRY-FREE

8 ounces boneless stew meat (pork, beef, or lamb), cut into ½-inch pieces

2 cups kimchi, cut into ½-inch pieces

2 cups beef or chicken broth (such as on pages 176, 178) or water

1 cup chopped onion

1 cup dried shiitake mushrooms (see Cook's Note)

3 garlic cloves, sliced

1 (2-inch) piece peeled fresh ginger

1 tablespoon toasted sesame oil

1 tablespoon dark soy sauce or tamari (gluten-free soy sauce)

1 tablespoon gochujang (Korean chile paste) or sambal oelek (garlic-chile paste)

Pinch of coconut sugar or dark brown sugar

8 ounces semi-firm tofu, drained

Fine sea salt

4 scallions, white and green parts, thinly sliced; or pea shoots or other microgreens

I learned about kimchi and kimchi stew from my friend Lisa Kim when we worked together at *Oprah* magazine, both fresh from college. Lisa's mom would pack homemade, big-flavor Korean classics for Lisa's office lunch, which made even my most exciting cold containers of tossed green salads increasingly unappealing. Lisa introduced me to the best Korean markets and restaurants in New York City, inspiring me to make my own Kimchi Jigae. Now, when I'm hankering for big spices that will knock my socks off, this stew is my go-to. It's alive with heat and fermented kimchi, which together will kick your immune system into high gear. This is delicious right out of the gate, but it gets more and more flavorful each day and every time you reheat it.

1. Combine the meat, kimchi, broth, onion, mushrooms, garlic, ginger, sesame oil, soy sauce, chile paste, and coconut sugar in the inner pot of the pressure cooker. Lock on the lid and Pressure Cook on high pressure for 15 minutes. Release the pressure naturally (if time allows, for maximum tenderness) or manually.

2. Meanwhile, cut the tofu into ½- to 1-inch cubes. Open the lid. Stir in the tofu, place the lid back on, and let sit on the Keep Warm setting until the tofu is warmed through, 3 to 5 minutes.

3. Open the lid. Taste and season with salt as needed. Spoon the stew into bowls and top with the scallions.

No Mushrooms? No Problem: Let's say you have a hankering for kimchi soup, but you don't have dried mushrooms at home. You can get away with skipping them for the beef or lamb version, but don't skip the mushrooms on the vegetarian version—they're needed for body *and* flavor here.

NOTES ON BROTH

One of the pleasant surprises about the pressure cooker is that flavor builds quickly under pressure, even if you're using water instead of chicken, pork, or beef broth. Of course, if you have homemade or high-quality prepared broth at the ready, using it will only improve the total deliciousness of your soup. But for soups and stews that call for bone-in meat, water works in a pinch.

For vegetable- and bean-based soups, I find starting with homemade chicken or vegetable broth yields the best taste. Take the time to make low-cost, low-work vegetable broth from scratch on occasion (see page 174) so you have it on hand when you need it.

TRY THIS! VEGETARIAN KIMCHI AND TOFU STEW
(DAIRY-FREE VEGETARIAN)

Make as described, but omit the meat and double the amount
of tofu, shiitake mushrooms, sesame oil, and soy sauce.

BEANS, VEGETABLES + OTHER SIDES

Here's a selection of fast, filling, healthy-ish sides that can become a meal when paired with lots of the other dishes in this book—and just about anything else you already make (think: steamed fish, seared chicken, pork chops . . .). None of these recipes takes much time, and all can be adjusted to your liking. You'll find fluffy Coconut-Turmeric Rice (page 102), Creamy Parmesan Polenta (page 89), infinitely repeatable Marinated Picnic Beans (page 84) with bursts of tomatoes and herbs, and tasty, tender vegetables in every size, shape, and color—all of them ready in no time flat.

Dreamy, Creamy (Any-Bean) Hummus

MAKES ABOUT 2½ CUPS
GLUTEN-FREE DAIRY-FREE
VEGAN VEGETARIAN

2 cups cooked chickpeas
(see page 181) or cannellini
beans (see page 181)

1 garlic clove

¼ cup tahini

5 tablespoons lemon juice
(from 1 large lemon)

1½ teaspoons ground coriander

1 teaspoon fine sea salt, plus
more as needed

¼ cup extra-virgin olive oil

I know, *many* of you probably buy your hummus from the store. I admit, with so many good ones out there, it's hard to get inspired to make it yourself. But here's the deal: in a pressure cooker, you can make the creamiest, dreamiest hummus from scratch, and lots of it, on the cheap and quicker than you think. What's more, hummus is *way* more than just a dip. It's a bed for golden meatballs or gorgeous steamed carrots. It's a dip, a side dish, a starter, and a topper all at once. So dive into this—you won't be disappointed. Once you've mastered cooking chickpeas or cannellini beans, know that you can make a variation of hummus with just about any other bean or even lentils.

Pulse the beans, garlic, tahini, lemon juice, coriander, and 1 teaspoon salt in a food processor until smooth, scraping the bowl occasionally. Gradually add the olive oil, pulsing to make a super-smooth paste. Season with additional salt as desired.

THINGS TO DO WITH HUMMUS

We all know we can serve hummus as a starter with crudités for dipping. But once you have that luscious, creamy dip in your arsenal, you can use it for so much more. Here are a few ideas:

- as a bed for Honey-Braised Carrots (page 88)
- as a base for turkey meatballs (see Turkey Meatball Soup with Macaroni and Kale, page 69), topped with shaved celery and shaved parmesan
- garnished with Fennel-Roasted Chickpeas (see page 64) and a scattering of herbs and oil
- piled with juicy pulled pork (see page 125) or Quick Pork Bolognese for a Crowd (page 122) and fresh pea shoots

Marinated Picnic Beans

PREP TIME: 10 MINUTES
TOTAL TIME: 1 HOUR 10
MINUTES (plus soaking time)
SERVES 8
GLUTEN-FREE DAIRY-FREE
VEGAN* VEGETARIAN*

1 pound dried chickpeas, cannellini beans, Corona beans, or large heirloom beans (such as Scarlet Runner), picked over and rinsed (about 2 cups)

7 cups chicken or vegetable broth (such as on pages 178, 174) or water *For vegan and vegetarian, use vegetable broth or water

1 small onion, halved

2 garlic cloves, smashed

1 teaspoon fine sea salt, plus more as needed

1 teaspoon fennel seeds

1 or 2 sprigs fresh rosemary, oregano, or thyme

Pinch of sweet paprika, smoked paprika, or pimentón (Spanish paprika)

⅓ cup extra-virgin olive oil

3 tablespoons apple cider vinegar

FOR SERVING

½ teaspoon red pepper flakes or 1 small green chile, such as jalapeño or serrano, thinly sliced

½ packed cup fresh dill, parsley, mint, or a combination

1 cup halved cherry or grape tomatoes; or 1 large beefsteak or heirloom tomato, cored and chopped

1 lemon, halved

Cool or room-temperature bean salads are a summer classic. Yes, they're easy to throw together with canned beans that require no cooking, but when you cook dried beans in the pressure cooker, they become more creamy and flavorful. Then, with the lightest of dressings, these same beans are marinated and ready to be spooned over Perfect Toast (see box, page 48), served alongside barbecued chicken, or to go elbow-to-elbow with an ear of sweet corn. It's picnic and potluck food at its best. Before you start, note the soaking time; for best results, don't skip it, and add salt as needed.

1. Soak the beans for 10 to 12 hours in enough water to cover. Drain and rinse. (Alternatively, use the quick-soak method; see page 180.)

2. Place the beans in the inner pot of the pressure cooker. Add the broth, onion, garlic, 1 teaspoon salt, fennel seeds, herbs, and paprika. Lock on the lid and Pressure Cook on high pressure for 15 to 20 minutes, depending on the type of bean (see bean cooking chart, page 181).

3. Let the pressure release naturally (about 20 minutes), then open the lid and turn off the cooker. (Don't leave it on the Keep Warm setting, as the beans may overcook and become mushy.) Drain the beans and let cool completely in a large bowl.

4. In a small bowl, whisk together the olive oil and vinegar. Pour over the beans and toss to coat well. (At this point, you can refrigerate the beans in a covered container for up to 4 days, if desired.)

5. To serve, toss the beans with the red pepper flakes, herbs, tomatoes, and additional salt as needed. Squeeze the lemon halves over the top.

TRY THIS! WARM WINTER BEANS WITH PISTOU
(GLUTEN-FREE VEGETARIAN)

Mix an extra 1 to 2 tablespoons olive oil into a ¼-cup batch of Garlicky Pistou (see page 54). Follow the recipe for Marinated Picnic Beans through step 2. Open the lid and spoon out the beans, reserving up to 2½ cups of the warm bean cooking liquid to loosen the beans. Skip the vinaigrette and instead serve the beans saucy and warm, with a generous dollop of pistou swirled or stirred in.

Lemon, Garlic, and Parmesan Spaghetti Squash

PREP TIME: 10 MINUTES
TOTAL TIME: 40 MINUTES
SERVES 4 TO 6
GLUTEN-FREE VEGETARIAN

1 small spaghetti squash (about 2 pounds), halved lengthwise and seeded

1 teaspoon flaky sea salt, such as Maldon, plus more as needed

½ teaspoon freshly ground black pepper

Pinch of red pepper flakes (optional)

2 garlic cloves, thinly sliced

2 tablespoons extra-virgin olive oil, plus more for serving

Zest of 1 lemon

½ cup finely grated parmesan cheese

There's something magically satisfying about spaghetti squash when it's cooked *just right* and seasoned well. It satisfies the craving for carby mouthfuls and takes on just about any flavors you want to give it. My family loves spaghetti squash with a lemon, garlic, and parmesan treatment that never grows old and works well on other types of squash, too.

1. Sprinkle the halved squash with the 1 teaspoon salt, ½ teaspoon black pepper, red pepper flakes (if using), and garlic, and then drizzle with 2 tablespoons olive oil. Set the squash in the inner pot of the pressure cooker and add about ¾ cup water to the pot. Lock on the lid and Pressure Cook on high pressure for 12 minutes.

2. Release the pressure naturally (about 10 minutes), then open the lid. Set the pot aside until the squash is cool enough to handle. (The squash should be completely tender but still hold its shape.)

3. Remove the squash from the pot and use a fork to comb the strands loose from the skin. Transfer the squash strands to a platter or bowl. Add the lemon zest, drizzle with a little additional olive oil, and sprinkle with the parmesan. Toss well to coat. Sprinkle with more salt and pepper, as desired.

Butter-Braised Radishes

PREP TIME: 5 MINUTES
TOTAL TIME: 20 MINUTES
SERVES 4 TO 6
GLUTEN-FREE VEGETARIAN

2 bunches radishes (globe,
breakfast, Easter Egg, or purple
daikon radish), scrubbed,
trimmed, and halved

1 teaspoon sherry vinegar or
apple cider vinegar

4 tablespoons unsalted butter

FOR SERVING

1 teaspoon flaky sea salt,
such as Maldon

½ teaspoon freshly ground
black pepper

¼ cup fresh dill, roughly chopped

Pinch of fennel seeds

On paper, it would seem only an epicure could be seduced by braised radishes. But you haven't lived until you've tried these. The radishes' signature bite is tempered by heat (and pressure), revealing a clean, juicy-tender spring side that's beautiful with fish or chicken or even tossed into a grain bowl or green salad. These are, admittedly, a grown-up flavor, but give them a shot—even if only on those nights when the adults gather after the kids are already in bed.

1. Place the radishes, about ⅓ cup water, the vinegar, and butter in the inner pot of the pressure cooker. Lock on the lid and Pressure Cook on high pressure for 12 minutes.

2. Open the lid and transfer the radishes to a platter. Serve warm, seasoned with the flaky sea salt and black pepper and sprinkled with the dill and fennel seeds.

BUTTER-BRAISED RADISHES AND
HONEY-BRAISED CARROTS (PAGE 88)

Honey-Braised Carrots

PREP TIME: 5 MINUTES
TOTAL TIME: 20 MINUTES
SERVES 4 TO 6
GLUTEN-FREE DIARY-FREE*
VEGETARIAN

2 bunches small carrots of
roughly equal size (about
2 pounds), scrubbed, greens
trimmed to 1 inch

2 tablespoons unsalted butter
or extra-virgin olive oil

1 tablespoon honey

½ teaspoon fine sea salt

½ teaspoon freshly ground black
pepper

FOR SERVING

½ packed cup fresh parsley, mint,
dill, oregano, or a combination,
roughly chopped

1 teaspoon flaky sea salt,
such as Maldon

As a kid, I loved the honey-glazed carrots that graced my grandmother's table: the same style as showed up at weddings, funerals, and at Cracker Barrel—everywhere except at home (my mom was more the broccoli or snap-pea type). I was determined to make those carrots—easy and satisfying, and just a touch sweet—a part of my family table. Some nights, they make dinnertime go more smoothly (if you're a parent, you know what I mean).

To me, the most alluring carrots aren't those cut into rounds or those baby carrots from the bag. I prefer full-length farmer's market beauties, lanky and bursting with flavor (many supermarkets now carry tricolor carrots). A simple scrub readies these carrots for a quick steam-cook, followed by an easy glaze of butter and honey. It's a dish you'll return to again and again.

1. Place the carrots, about ¼ cup of water, the butter, honey, ½ teaspoon salt, and ½ teaspoon pepper in the inner pot of the pressure cooker. Pressure Cook on high pressure for 3 minutes for smaller carrots or 5 minutes for larger ones. Release the pressure manually and open the lid. The carrots should be somewhere between al dente and completely tender. Use a slotted spoon to transfer the carrots to a plate. Keep warm.

2. Use the Saute function to reduce the cooking liquid until thickened to your liking (I like it thick enough to lightly coat a spoon), 2 to 3 minutes.

3. Spoon the carrots onto a serving platter and drizzle some of the sauce over the top. Garnish with the herbs and flaky salt.

Creamy Parmesan Polenta

PREP TIME: 5 MINUTES
TOTAL TIME: 25 MINUTES
SERVES 4
GLUTEN-FREE VEGETARIAN*

4 cups chicken or vegetable broth (pages 178, 174) or water
  *For vegetarian, use vegetable broth

1 cup polenta (coarse cornmeal) or grits (not quick-cooking)

1⅓ cups finely grated parmesan cheese (4 ounces), plus more for serving

4 tablespoons (½ stick) unsalted butter

½ teaspoon fine sea salt

Whole milk, as needed

Freshly ground black pepper

Few things are more satisfying than a bowl of creamy, cheesy polenta or grits. It can form the base for that all-time Southern favorite, shrimp and grits. But it can serve as the bed for tender braised beef (try Double-the-Vegetables Pot Roast, page 129), and it makes a wheat-free warm breakfast bowl when drizzled with maple syrup. This cheesy version is even fine and dandy all on its own as a side dish.

1. Place the broth and polenta in the inner pot of the pressure cooker. Lock on the lid and Pressure Cook on high pressure for 9 minutes. Release the pressure naturally (about 10 minutes), then open the lid. The polenta should be thick and no longer gritty.

2. Stir in the parmesan, butter, and salt. Leave on the Keep Warm setting until ready to serve.

3. Just before serving, loosen the polenta with a little milk, if needed. Serve the polenta in bowls, garnished with pepper and more parmesan.

FOR THE SLOW COOKER

Make the polenta as instructed in step 1, adding all the ingredients to the slow cooker. Cook on High for 2 hours, then proceed with step 2.

COOK'S NOTE

No-Dairy Dinner Side: Looking for a similarly creamy but vegan or dairy-free side? Skip the butter, milk, and cheese—add in warm vegetable broth or water to loosen, and stir in 2 tablespoons white miso paste for a cheese-like depth.

Fast Root-Vegetable Mash

PREP TIME: 10 MINUTES
TOTAL TIME: 35 MINUTES
SERVES 4 TO 6
GLUTEN-FREE VEGETARIAN

1 small cauliflower, halved,
   or 1 small celery root, peeled
   and halved

2 large russet potatoes, peeled

1 teaspoon flaky sea salt, such as
   Maldon, plus more as needed

⅓ cup finely grated parmesan
   cheese

3 to 4 tablespoons unsalted
   butter, plus more as needed
   (see Cook's Note)

¼ to ⅓ cup milk of choice (see
   Cook's Note)

Freshly ground black pepper

⅓ packed cup fresh dill, roughly
   chopped (optional)

COOK'S NOTE

A Creamy Mash: My crowd is a "more butter, more milk, please" bunch, so while I've given a range on the milk and butter, I do use 4 tablespoons butter and the full ⅓ cup milk. You might prefer less, or more, or go dairy-free with nondairy milk and butter.

Deceptively mashed potato-like, these root vegetables offer a lot more fiber and nutrients but the same belly-warming, comforting qualities. For the fluffiest finish with notes of buttery mashed potatoes, I like to use a mix of vegetables and potatoes, but once you get the hang of this, you can mix and match to your taste. If you're skeptical, know that a little parmesan, butter, and salt goes a long way toward making absolutely every vegetable tasty (even the most cauliflower-hating vegetable sleuth will gobble this down).

1.   Place the cauliflower, potatoes, about 1 cup water, and 1 teaspoon salt in the inner pot of the pressure cooker; you may need to quarter some of the vegetables, depending on the size of your cooker. Lock on the lid and Pressure Cook on high pressure for 20 minutes. Release the pressure naturally (about 20 minutes) or manually and open the lid. The vegetables should be fork-tender.

2.   Drain and transfer the vegetables to a large bowl and, while still hot, mash with the parmesan and butter, adding a little milk to lighten, if desired. (A potato masher will work fine here if you like a chunky mash, or use a ricer for a perfectly creamy, no-lump mash.) Season the mash with salt and pepper to taste.

3.   Serve warm, garnished with additional flaky sea salt, the dill (if using), and more butter if you like.

Maple-Cinnamon Squash Agrodolce

PREP TIME: 10 MINUTES
TOTAL TIME: 30 MINUTES
SERVES 4 TO 6
GLUTEN-FREE DAIRY-FREE*
VEGAN* VEGETARIAN

2 small winter squash, halved and seeded (or quartered to fit, if large)

1 teaspoon flaky sea salt, such as Maldon

½ teaspoon freshly ground black pepper

Pinch of red pepper flakes

¼ teaspoon ground cinnamon

1 tablespoon extra-virgin olive oil

¾ cup water

3 tablespoons pure maple syrup

1 tablespoon apple cider vinegar

2 tablespoons unsalted butter
*For dairy-free and vegan, use a dairy-free butter substitute

One of my earliest food memories is of my mom's baked acorn squash, with pools of brown-sugary butter floating in its roomy cavity—an American classic. It set in motion a deep and lifelong love affair with winter squash that has served me well. Squash is inexpensive, nutrient-dense, and easy—though time-intensive—to prepare. I've tweaked my mom's recipe for a quicker weeknight side dish with a touch of *agrodolce* (Italian for "sour and sweet") thanks to a blend of cider vinegar and maple syrup, so the squash, not brown sugar, is front and center.

My favorite squash variety for this treatment is Delicata, a delicate (as the name suggests) striated squash you can eat skin and all; but any smallish winter variety, like sweet dumpling, carnival, ambercup, or the classic acorn, will do.

1. Sprinkle the squash with the flaky salt, black pepper, red pepper flakes, and cinnamon; drizzle with the olive oil and then add to the inner pot of the pressure cooker, layering as needed. Add the water to the pot. Lock on the lid and Pressure Cook on high pressure for 12 minutes.

2. Release the pressure naturally (about 10 minutes), then open the lid. Set the inner pot aside until the squash is just cool enough to handle (the squash should be completely tender but still hold its shape). Transfer the squash to a platter and keep warm.

3. Add the maple syrup and cider vinegar to the liquid in the inner pot. Set the pressure cooker to Saute and cook until slightly reduced and thickened, about 8 minutes. Stir in the butter to emulsify.

4. Drizzle the sauce over the squash and serve.

TRY THIS! VEGAN COCONUT SQUASH
WITH TOASTED WALNUTS AND POMEGRANATE
(GLUTEN-FREE DAIRY-FREE VEGAN VEGETARIAN)

Prepare the squash, omitting the cinnamon and using coconut oil instead of butter. Top the cooked squash with toasted walnuts, flaky sea salt, and roughly chopped fresh parsley. Squeeze some lemon juice generously over the top and serve sprinkled with pomegranate seeds.

No-Fuss Steamed Beets
with Parsley Herb-Caper Vinaigrette

PREP TIME: 5 MINUTES
TOTAL TIME: 55 MINUTES
SERVES 4 TO 6
GLUTEN-FREE DAIRY-FREE*
VEGAN* VEGETARIAN

2 bunches (about 2 pounds) beets (red, golden, or a mix), scrubbed and trimmed

¼ cup extra-virgin olive oil

2 tablespoons sherry vinegar or apple cider vinegar

1 teaspoon fine sea salt

½ teaspoon freshly ground black pepper

⅓ cup capers, drained

⅓ packed cup fresh dill, roughly chopped

⅓ packed cup fresh parsley, roughly chopped

FOR SERVING

Homemade Yogurt (page 160) or store-bought plain whole-milk yogurt *For dairy-free and vegan, use dairy-free yogurt

Toasted hazelnuts (or any nuts), roughly chopped

Flaky sea salt, such as Maldon

This bracing side dish—a perfect accompaniment to anything meaty, fatty, cheesy, gooey, or bready—is a chore under normal circumstances, because beets are messy to peel and time-consuming to roast or steam. But as you've learned by now, cooking with a pressure cooker is not exactly normal circumstances. You can just scrub the beets (no peeling!) and steam them whole (I use a steamer basket, but if you don't have one, just add the beets directly to the pot). Then you can slip the skins right off before slicing the beets and tossing them in oil and vinegar. Give them a gloriously fresh finish with hazelnuts, capers, and herbs.

1. Place the beets in the steamer basket and set the basket into the inner pot of the pressure cooker. (If you don't have a steamer basket, just add the beets directly to the cooker.) Pour in about 1 cup water, and Pressure Cook on high pressure for 20 minutes for small beets and 25 minutes for large ones. Let the pressure release naturally (about 20 minutes) or release it manually, then open the lid. Remove the beets from the pot—they should be fork-tender—and let cool until easy to handle.

2. Whisk together the olive oil, vinegar, salt, and pepper in a large bowl. Stir in the capers, dill, and parsley.

3. Slip the beets out of their skins, and slice into halves or quarters. Add the beets to the dressing and toss to combine.

4. Spread a few spoonfuls of yogurt on a platter or serving plates, and spoon the dressed beets over the top, sprinkling them with hazelnuts and flaky salt. Serve at room temperature. (You can refrigerate the steamed beets, dressed or not, in an airtight container for up to 1 week.)

Creamed Mexican Street Corn

(ESQUITE)

PREP TIME: 5 MINUTES
TOTAL TIME: 30 MINUTES
SERVES 4 TO 6
GLUTEN-FREE VEGETARIAN

6 ears fresh corn, kernels
   scraped, or 6 cups frozen
   corn kernels (from
   2 [16-ounce] bags)

¾ cup water

1 small shallot, minced

2 teaspoons cornstarch

2 tablespoons unsalted butter

1 teaspoon fine sea salt

1 cup half-and-half or
   almond-milk creamer

½ cup grated parmesan, plus
   extra for serving

FOR SERVING

Freshly cracked black
   peppercorns

Cayenne

1 firm-ripe avocado, peeled and
   quartered (optional)

Lime wedges

Short of a classic fresh ear of buttered corn, my favorite way to eat corn is inspired by my travels to Mexico, where I had it with plenty of cheese, cayenne, and a big squeeze of lime in a market outside Mexico City. This is a creamy, spoonable version—as quick and easy as it gets—and a no-nonsense side dish for any time of the year.

1. Place the corn kernels, water, shallot, cornstarch, butter, and salt in the inner pot of the pressure cooker. Lock on the lid and Pressure Cook on high pressure for 3 minutes. Let the steam release naturally.

2. Open the lid and stir in the half-and-half and parmesan. Cook further on the Saute setting to thicken the cream if desired, about 2 minutes.

3. Serve the creamy corn warm, sprinkled with black pepper and cayenne, topped with the avocado, and with a lime wedge on the side.

TRY THIS! CREAMED CORN RISOTTO

Got leftover creamed corn? Stir it into Cacio e Pepe Risotto (page 107) and reheat on the stovetop for a quick next-day corn-and-parmesan risotto.

COOK'S NOTE

Almost-Instant Corn on the Cob: Prefer your corn on the cob? A pressure cooker can make quick work of it. Here's how: Place 4 to 6 husked ears (silks also removed) on a trivet, set the trivet into the pressure cooker, and add 1 cup water (break longer ears in half for smaller pressure cookers). Lock on the lid and Pressure Cook on high pressure for 2 minutes. Release the pressure manually, then open the lid and remove the ears. Serve warm with butter or with grated parmesan, cayenne, and lime wedges on the side for your crowd to garnish as desired.

Refried Beans

PREP TIME: 15 MINUTES
TOTAL TIME: 1 HOUR 30 MINUTES
SERVES 8 TO 10
GLUTEN-FREE DAIRY-FREE

1 pound dried pinto beans (about 2 cups), picked over and rinsed

7 cups chicken or vegetable broth (pages 178, 174)
*For vegan and vegetarian, use vegetable broth

1 small onion, chopped

3 garlic cloves, sliced

1 teaspoon fine sea salt

¾ teaspoon ground cumin

½ teaspoon dried oregano

½ teaspoon smoked paprika or cayenne

3 tablespoons cooking fat (coconut oil, olive oil, or bacon fat) *For dairy-free, vegan, and vegetarian, use coconut oil or olive oil

FOR SERVING

2 small green chiles, such as jalapeño or serrano, thinly sliced

Fresh cilantro leaves

Queso fresco or cotija cheese, crumbled

Sliced firm-ripe avocado

Lime wedges

Tortilla chips or warm tortillas, optional

Any day of the week, I can make my husband smile by handing him a warm bowl of refried beans sprinkled with cheese. It doesn't take much to please him, but as a longtime vegetarian, he finds a bowl of creamy beans to be earthy, satisfying bliss. We both like this dish best using pinto beans, and easy on the spices, but with enough fat (bacon fat, or coconut or olive oil for my vegetarian husband) to make it feel like a classic. Add chiles, cheese, cilantro, avocado, lime, and even tortillas to turn this staple into a meal.

1. Add the beans, broth, onion, garlic, salt, cumin, oregano, paprika, and fat of choice to the inner pot of the pressure cooker. Lock on the lid and Pressure Cook on high pressure for 45 minutes. Let the pressure release naturally (about 20 minutes), or manually release the pressure. Open the lid. Drain the beans, reserving their liquid.

2. Puree the beans with an immersion blender or in a food processor until smooth, adding the cooking liquid, ¼ cup at a time, until the beans reach your desired consistency. (I like mine with about 1 cup of bean broth, since the beans tighten as they cool.)

3. Serve warm or at room temperature, with the chiles, cilantro, cheese, avocado, and lime wedges for squeezing over the top.

FOR THE SLOW COOKER

Place all the step 1 ingredients for the refried beans in the slow cooker and cook on High for 2 to 4 hours or on Low for 6 hours. Then continue with step 2.

Coconut Plantains

PREP TIME: 5 MINUTES
TOTAL TIME: 20 MINUTES
SERVES 4 TO 6
GLUTEN-FREE DAIRY-FREE
VEGAN VEGETARIAN

2 tablespoons unsalted butter

2 tablespoons extra-virgin
coconut oil or canola oil

4 large very ripe yellow plantains
(about 2½ pounds; their skins
should be brown or black),
peeled and halved lengthwise

2 tablespoons coconut sugar or
light or dark brown sugar

¼ teaspoon ground cinnamon

¾ cup water

Flaky sea salt, such as Maldon

In the Caribbean and parts of Latin America and Africa, soft, toothsome sweet plantains (*maduros*) are a standard side dish, the perfect accompaniment for rice and beans, pulled pork, or chicken tacos. I like plantains with a little color on them (from caramelization), and I prefer them not greasy, with just a bit of bite left. This hands-off treatment yields tender, low-mess rewards.

1. Place the butter and oil in the inner pot of the pressure cooker and set to Saute. Once the butter is melted, add the plantains and stir to coat. Cook without stirring until browned on one side, 3 to 5 minutes. (The goal is just to get some nice browning, without breaking up the plantains or spending too much time on it.)

2. Add the coconut sugar and cinnamon and stir to coat; it's okay if a few plantains stick to the pot. Add the water, lock on the lid, and Pressure Cook on high pressure for 5 minutes.

3. Let the pressure release naturally (about 10 minutes), then release the remaining pressure manually. Open the lid. Spoon the plantains into bowls and serve warm, sprinkled with flaky salt.

Biryani Rice

PREP TIME: 15 MINUTES
TOTAL TIME: 26 MINUTES
SERVES 4
GLUTEN-FREE VEGETARIAN

1½ cups basmati rice

1 to 2 tablespoons ghee
  (clarified butter; see Cook's
  Note, page 66) or unsalted
  butter

1 bay leaf

1 cinnamon stick

½ teaspoon fennel seeds

1 small onion, chopped

2 garlic cloves, thinly sliced

1 teaspoon minced peeled fresh
  ginger

1¼ teaspoons ground coriander

1 teaspoon sweet paprika

½ teaspoon ground cumin

¼ teaspoon ground turmeric

Pinch of ground cardamom
  (optional)

1½ cups water

2 teaspoons fine sea salt

FOR SERVING

2 tablespoons golden raisins

½ cup roasted cashews, halved
  or roughly chopped

1 cup fresh cilantro and mint
  leaves, torn or roughly
  chopped

Biryani rice is a fragrant, mouthwatering Indian classic. It makes a beautiful side dish for Chicken Tikka Masala (page 111) or Simple Saag Paneer (page 126) or even a brilliant main course on its own (see variation that follows). A classic biryani takes a long time (and many dirty dishes) to pull off, but the pressure cooker makes quick work of this family favorite. A traditional biryani is heady with fragrant spices, but feel free to cut back or to skip any that don't speak to you.

1. Soak the rice in water for 15 minutes (see Cook's Note, page 102) and then rinse until the water runs clear; drain.

2. Place the ghee in the inner pot of the pressure cooker and set to Saute. Once the ghee is melted, add the bay leaf, cinnamon stick, and fennel seeds and toast, stirring, until fragrant, about 1 minute.

3. Add the onion to the inner pot and cook until softened, 6 to 8 minutes. Add the garlic, ginger, coriander, paprika, cumin, turmeric, and cardamom (if using) and cook, stirring, for another minute to toast the spices.

4. Add the drained rice, water, and salt to the inner pot; stir once. Lock on the lid and Pressure Cook on high pressure for 4 minutes. Release the pressure manually, and open the lid. The rice should be tender and fluffy. Discard the cinnamon stick and bay leaf.

5. Stir in the raisins and cashews, and sprinkle with the cilantro and mint. Serve warm.

TRY THIS! CHICKEN BIRYANI
(GLUTEN-FREE)

To make this into a main dish, add 1¼ pounds boneless, skinless chicken thighs, cut into 1-inch pieces, to the pot after sautéing the spices, then add the rice in step 4 and cook as described.

Coconut-Turmeric Rice
with Almonds and Herbs

PREP TIME: 15 MINUTES
TOTAL TIME: 40 MINUTES
(includes soaking)
SERVES 4
GLUTEN-FREE DAIRY-FREE
VEGAN VEGETARIAN

1½ cups basmati rice

1 bay leaf

1 teaspoon ground turmeric

1 (13.5-ounce) can unsweetened full-fat coconut milk

1 tablespoon coconut oil (optional)

Pinch of saffron (optional)

1 scant teaspoon fine sea salt

FOR SERVING

½ cup toasted sliced almonds

1 cup fresh cilantro and mint leaves, torn or roughly chopped

2 to 4 Persian cucumbers, sliced or halved lengthwise

1 lime, cut into wedges

So many people around the world have a take on this winning recipe of rice, infused with turmeric and coconut. In our house, it's a welcome escape from meat and potatoes land. It is light but satisfying, with vibrant color (thanks to the turmeric) and surprising textures—an easy side dish that never seems to get old. When a warm, soothing bowl of rice calls, here's the number.

1. Soak the rice in water for 15 minutes (see Cook's Note, below) and then rinse until the water runs clear; drain.

2. Add the rice, bay leaf, turmeric, coconut milk, coconut oil (if using), saffron (if using), and salt to the inner pot of the pressure cooker. Stir once or twice to distribute the spices. Lock on the lid and Pressure Cook on high pressure for 4 minutes. Release the pressure manually, then open the lid. The rice should be tender and fluffy. Discard the bay leaf.

3. Serve the rice warm, garnished with the almonds, cilantro and mint, cucumbers, and lime wedges.

COOK'S NOTE

Make It a Meal: For a one-pot vegetarian dinner, stir 2 cups roughly chopped chard or kale into the rice after cooking, or, sprinkle the warm rice with a handful of thinly sliced fresh snap peas and serve.

COOK'S NOTE

Why Soak the Rice? Soaking rice before cooking is thought to reduce toxic substances, like trace arsenic, and release them from the grains into the water. It's a good habit to soak rice for at least 15 minutes (and up to overnight) if you have time. Then rinse the rice until the water runs clear, and cook as directed. If you decide to skip soaking, add up to ¼ cup additional water to the rice when cooking.

ONE-POT
MAINS
+ MEALS

Raise your hand if you *still* don't know what's for dinner tonight! I'm with you. Even for a four-time cookbook author, dinner is the meal that too often sends panic crashing down on family life. But with a pressure cooker or slow cooker (and a dozen or so easy, repeatable recipes), an evening meal can quickly morph into a cue for the whole family to slow down and relax. Dinner should be a time of gathering, nourishing, and reconnecting, a time to fuel up and bring a little fun back into your family routine.

My magic dinner formula is *flavor + speed*. I like to make something filling and exciting, but that won't take all night to make—or clean up! (No one needs grumpy kids circling your legs while you work your way through a long ingredient list.) The recipes in this chapter are fast and straightforward, with any extra work tucked into the time it takes your cooker to pressurize.

Cacio e Pepe Risotto

PREP TIME: 15 MINUTES
TOTAL TIME: 50 MINUTES
SERVES 4
GLUTEN-FREE VEGETARIAN*

1 tablespoon extra-virgin olive oil

2 sprigs fresh sage, leaves picked

1 small onion, finely chopped

3 small garlic cloves, thinly sliced (optional)

2 cups Arborio rice, rinsed and drained

⅔ cup dry white wine, such as Sauvignon Blanc

5 cups chicken or vegetable broth (such as on pages 178, 174) *For vegetarian, use vegetable broth

½ teaspoon fine sea salt, plus more as needed

¾ to 1 cup grated pecorino romano, parmesan, or a blend, plus more for serving

3 tablespoons unsalted butter

Freshly ground black pepper

Pea shoots (optional)

If you make one thing from this book to give your pressure cooker a fair shot, make this. Risotto in a pressure cooker is a miracle—amazingly quick, bafflingly easy, and spot-on delicious. That creamy, comforting bowl of weeknight risotto no longer requires a lot of standing and stirring at the stove. In the pressure cooker, it becomes fast food at its very best: hands-off (mostly) and easy to tweak. Here, the classic Italian pairing of cheese and black pepper is embellished with crispy sage. Once you master the basics, give yourself the freedom to play: try fresh pea shoots, crispy mushrooms, peas and asparagus, chunks of braised beef . . . the world is your oyster.

1.   Pour the olive oil into the inner pot of the pressure cooker and set to Saute. Add the sage leaves and cook until lightly crisp, 2 to 3 minutes. Remove with a slotted spoon and place on a paper towel–lined plate to drain.

2.   Add the onion, garlic, and rice to the inner pot (this is one time I skip soaking my rice!) and stir to coat in the sage-infused oil. Stir in the wine and cook until it evaporates a little, about 1 minute. Add the broth and ½ teaspoon salt.

3.   Lock on the lid and Pressure Cook on high pressure for 6 minutes. Release the pressure manually and open the lid. The rice should be tender and have absorbed most of the liquid, but should still seem a little loose.

4.   Stir in ½ cup of the cheese and the butter. The risotto will tighten as it cools. Serve warm, sprinkled with additional salt to taste, a generous helping of more cheese, and plenty of black pepper. Garnish with the crispy sage leaves and the pea shoots (if using).

COOK'S NOTE

Top Your Bowl: This main dish is soothing and comforting with the parmesan and pepper, but you can also stir in (or top with) shaved Brussels sprouts, sautéed mushrooms, finely sliced kale leaves, or even shaved radishes. Let your imagination run wild!

FOR THE SLOW COOKER

Add all the ingredients except the sage, cheese, and butter to the slow cooker and stir to blend. Cover and cook on High for 3 hours or on Low for 6 hours. Stir in the cheese and butter, adding a bit more broth to loosen, if needed. Serve warm, topped with salt to taste, more cheese, and the pepper.

COOK'S NOTE

Delay Start: Risotto is a perfect candidate for using the Delay Start time settings, allowing you to set the start of the cooking so it is completed when you're ready for it. If you don't plan to serve the risotto right away, you can cook the rice for 5 minutes instead of the 6 (the extra minute makes a difference!), and have it cook further while the steam slowly releases. But don't leave it on Keep Warm setting for longer than 5 minutes, or the rice will fall apart.

Easy Eggplant Parmesan

PREP TIME: 10 MINUTES
TOTAL TIME: 30 MINUTES
SERVES 6
GLUTEN-FREE VEGETARIAN

2 medium eggplants (about 2½ pounds), cut into ½-inch rounds

5 tablespoons extra-virgin olive oil

1 teaspoon fine sea salt

½ teaspoon freshly ground black pepper, plus more as needed

4 cups Quick Pomodoro Sauce (page 173) or store-bought marinara sauce

Red pepper flakes (optional)

1 pound capellini, linguine, or spaghetti

8 ounces fresh mozzarella, cut into rounds

¼ cup freshly grated parmesan cheese, plus more for serving

Fresh basil leaves

TRY THIS! ONE-POT PASTA DINNER (VEGETARIAN)

For making this an all-in-one-pot dinner, butter the inner pot of the pressure cooker, then spoon in the first cup of sauce and add 12 ounces of a short, chunky pasta (such as penne). Add the eggplant as instructed, as well as the remaining sauce; the pasta will cook in the tomato sauce and absorb extra liquid while the eggplant softens.

There are a few things a pressure cooker *can't* achieve, and crispy-skinned, golden-brown roast chicken, and bubbly, blistered eggplant parmesan are two of them. So you need to adjust your expectations a bit here. But if you want a light, fresh, and extremely easy eggplant parm moment—say, for ballet Tuesdays or soccer Saturdays—in 30 minutes instead of 1½ hours, this will more than do the trick. (Strict Italophiles, move along.) If you're attached to the blistered cheese and don't mind washing an extra pan, gently transfer the contents of the pot to a shallow casserole and brown under the broiler.

Also, here you cook the pasta in a separate pot so as to serve the eggplant parm with a long pasta (the 10 minutes' Pressure Cook time is too long for skinny pasta), but if penne's your game, substitute that to make this an all-in-one-pot meal (see One-Pot Pasta Dinner option that follows).

1. In a bowl, toss the eggplant slices with the olive oil and sprinkle with the salt and ½ teaspoon pepper.

2. Add a generous cup of the tomato sauce to inner pot of the pressure cooker, spreading it to cover the bottom. Layer in about half the eggplant rounds (no need to be exact). Spoon over another generous cup of sauce, followed by a second layer of eggplant. Sprinkle with some red pepper flakes, if desired. Pour over the remaining 2 cups sauce. Lock on the lid and Pressure Cook on high pressure for 10 minutes.

3. Meanwhile, cook the pasta in a large pot of boiling salt water according to the package directions.

4. Manually release the pressure from the cooker (or let it first release naturally for 5 minutes), then open the lid. The eggplant should be completely tender. Add the mozzarella and parmesan and return the lid without locking it (any cheese that touches the sides will trigger a burn notice). Let sit on the Keep Warm setting until the cheese is melted, 4 to 5 minutes.

5. Divide the pasta among plates and spoon the eggplant parmesan and extra sauce over the top. Season with some more pepper, sprinkle with more parmesan, and garnish with the basil leaves.

Stuffed Sweet Potato "Tacos"

PREP TIME: 10 MINUTES
TOTAL TIME: 25 MINUTES
SERVES 4
GLUTEN-FREE VEGETARIAN

4 large sweet potatoes
(2¼ to 2½ pounds scrubbed)

1 cup cooked black beans (see
bean cooking chart, page 181);
or 1 (15.5-ounce) can black
beans, drained and warmed

1 cup shredded cheese, such as
mozzarella, Cheddar, or
Colby Jack

FOR SERVING

1 or 2 firm-ripe avocados, peeled
and sliced

1 green chile, such as jalapeño
or serrano, seeded and
thinly sliced

Fresh cilantro leaves

Fresh salsa or Pico de Gallo
(see page 131)

TRY THIS! QUICK CHILE-LIME
SWEET POTATOES
(GLUTEN-FREE DAIRY-FREE VEGAN
VEGETARIAN)

Want soft sweet potatoes for a quick
weeknight side? Cut 1 to 2 pounds
small sweet potatoes in half and
steam them for 16 minutes (using the
method at right). Serve warm, with
insides smashed with butter and
sprinkled with salt and a pinch of red
pepper flakes, then add a dash of
lime juice. Scatter with cilantro leaves,
if desired.

During the cooler months, my kids and I often eat a sweet potato each, if not more, at least once a week for a nutritious and tasty meal. Steamed to soft perfection in a pressure cooker, sweet potatoes are quick and filling, creamy and delicious. What's so amazing about mastering the quick-steam method here is that the sweet potatoes become the perfect blank slate for almost any toppings you love, including some of the sauces and fixings right here in this book. Our go-to treat is to have the sweet potatoes taco-style, with all the beans, avocado, and cheese we love so much in a tortilla, but you can stuff yours with Fennel-Roasted Chickpeas (page 64), pulled pork (page 125), Pico de Gallo (page 131), turkey meatballs (page 69), Quick Pomodoro Sauce (page 173), or Simple Saag Paneer (page 126).

If you want your toppings melty and toasty, it's easiest to transfer the sweet potatoes to a sheet pan, add the toppings, and quickly broil them. (Trying to put the stuffed sweet potatoes back into the pressure cooker is more trouble than it's worth.) These will have your family coming back for more.

1. Prick the sweet potatoes all over with a fork and place them in a steamer basket or on a trivet (stacking the potatoes if needed), then set into the inner pot of the pressure cooker. Pour about 6 cups water into the pot.

2. Lock on the lid and Pressure Cook on high pressure for 20 to 25 minutes, depending on the size of the sweet potatoes. Let the pressure release naturally (10 to 12 minutes) to give the potatoes time to get super creamy and soft. (Use this hands-off time to prep the toppings.)

3. Open the lid and let the sweet potatoes sit until cool enough to handle. Remove the potatoes from the pressure cooker and split them lengthwise down the middle with a sharp knife. Squeeze the edges to open slightly, then mash the insides with a fork.

4. Stuff the sweet potatoes with your favorite combination (we love warm beans and cheese). Serve warm, topped with avocado, jalapeño, cilantro, and salsa (kind of like tacos or chili!), or any of your favorite toppings.

Chicken Tikka Masala

PREP TIME: 20 MINUTES
TOTAL TIME: 1 HOUR
SERVES 4 TO 6
GLUTEN-FREE DAIRY-FREE*

½ cup ghee (clarified butter; see Cook's Note, page 66) or unsalted butter *For dairy-free, use coconut oil

1 medium onion, finely chopped

3 garlic cloves, thinly sliced

3 tablespoons minced peeled fresh ginger

1 teaspoon ground chile

2 teaspoons ground cumin

1 teaspoon sweet paprika

1 heaping tablespoon ground turmeric

1 (28-ounce) can whole peeled tomatoes

1 cinnamon stick

1¼ teaspoons fine sea salt, plus more as needed

2½ to 3 pounds boneless, skinless chicken thighs, cut into 1-inch pieces

¾ cup half-and-half or full-fat coconut milk

1 tablespoon fresh lemon juice

FOR SERVING

Cooked basmati rice or naan

4 scallions, white and green parts thinly sliced

½ cup fresh cilantro leaves

Homemade Yogurt (page 160) or store-bought plain yogurt or Cucumber Raita (see page 131)

In the world of make-at-home Indian food, this chicken dish reigns supreme. Making it in a pressure cooker takes a fraction of the normal time, but it requires *just a touch* of babysitting, since to get textures right you must cook the onions, tomatoes, and spices first, and the chicken later. But the big flavors you get as a reward are worth it. If you're looking for a juicy, big-flavor dinner that's fast, this simplified version of a classic is your winning ticket. To lean this recipe more plant-based, add in cauliflower florets or canned chickpeas (rinsed and drained) in place of half of the chicken, or try the tofu or paneer option below.

1. Place the ghee in the inner pot of the pressure cooker and set to Saute. Add the onion and cook until translucent, about 5 minutes. Add the garlic, ginger, ground chile, cumin, paprika, and turmeric and cook for 1 to 2 minutes more, stirring, until the spices are fragrant.

2. Add the tomatoes and their juices, the cinnamon stick, and 1½ teaspoons salt. Lock on the lid and Pressure Cook on high pressure for 3 minutes. Release the pressure manually and open the lid. The tomatoes and onion should be completely soft. Discard the cinnamon stick.

3. Puree the sauce with an immersion blender or mash it with a potato masher until mostly smooth. Stir in the chicken and lock on the lid again. Pressure Cook on high pressure for 5 minutes. Release the pressure manually and open the lid.

4. Stir in the half-and-half, replace the lid, and leave on the Keep Warm setting until ready to serve.

5. Open the lid. Add the lemon juice. Taste, and add more salt if needed. Serve over rice, with the scallions and cilantro scattered on top and yogurt or raita on the side.

TRY THIS! TOFU (OR PANEER) TIKKA MASALA
(GLUTEN-FREE VEGETARIAN)

Replace the chicken with 2 (16-ounce) containers firm tofu, drained and cut into ½-inch pieces, or 1½ pounds paneer, cubed. Stir in with the half-and-half at the end, to warm through.

Stovetop-Style Mac 'n' Cheese

PREP TIME: 5 MINUTES
TOTAL TIME: 25 MINUTES
SERVES 6 TO 8
VEGETARIAN

3 tablespoons unsalted butter

1 medium onion, finely chopped (optional)

1 pound short pasta, such as shells or elbows

4 cups chicken or vegetable broth (such as on pages 178, 174)

2 tightly packed cups shredded Cheddar-jack-mozzarella cheese blend

1¼ tightly packed cups shredded Gruyère, sharp Cheddar, or Gouda

¼ cup grated parmesan cheese

½ cup whole milk

2 teaspoons Dijon mustard (optional)

½ teaspoon freshly ground black pepper, plus more as needed

Fine sea salt

Pinch of paprika (optional)

Quick, creamy mac 'n' cheese that doesn't come out of a box is a godsend for family life, especially if you've got kids coming from and going to after-school activities—or you just need a comforting, crowd-pleasing meal and you need it quick! In no more time than it takes to peel open a cardboard box and measure out milk for powdered cheese, you can have this from-scratch version on the table.

1. Add the butter, onion (if using), pasta, and broth to the inner pot of the pressure cooker. Lock on the lid and Pressure Cook on high pressure for 6 minutes. Release the pressure manually (be careful—it will sputter; cover the valve with a cloth to catch some of the mess).

2. Open the lid and stir in all the cheese, the milk, mustard (if using), and ½ teaspoon pepper. Add salt to taste.

3. Let the pasta stand in the cooker on the Keep Warm setting for 5 minutes to thicken slightly. Serve warm, with a sprinkle of extra pepper and the paprika, if desired.

COOK'S NOTE

Bubbly Cheese-Topped Mac: If you like your mac 'n' cheese *full-on* in the cheese department, transfer the finished dish to a buttered 2-quart casserole, preheat the broiler and cover the casserole with 4 thin slices sharp Cheddar, mozzarella, or a mix of the two. Place on the lower rack and broil until the cheese is bubbly and golden.

COOK'S NOTE

Craving a Golden Cracker: If you're in the *crispy bread-crumb topping* camp regarding your mac 'n' cheese, this make-ahead is for you. Preheat the broiler. Combine 1 cup panko bread crumbs with 2 tablespoons melted butter in a small bowl. Spread out on a sheet pan and broil until golden brown, 1 to 2 minutes. Let the crumbs cool completely, then use or store in an airtight container for up to 5 weeks. This topping is great sprinkled over mac 'n' cheese but also on creamy beans or atop perfect soft-boiled eggs.

Red Curry Shrimp
with Basil and Lime

PREP TIME: 15 MINUTES
TOTAL TIME: 15 MINUTES
SERVES 4 TO 6
GLUTEN-FREE DAIRY-FREE

1½ pounds peeled and deveined medium shrimp

1 teaspoon fine sea salt

¼ teaspoon freshly ground black pepper

2 tablespoons coconut oil or canola oil

1 red chile, such as red serrano or Fresno, thinly sliced

1 (2-inch) piece fresh ginger, peeled and cut into coins

2 tablespoons red curry paste

1 (13.5-ounce) can unsweetened full-fat coconut milk

1 tablespoon soy sauce or tamari (gluten-free soy sauce)

1 teaspoon fish sauce (optional)

FOR SERVING

Cooked jasmine or other long-grain white rice

2 packed cups fresh basil, cilantro, or a combination

Lime wedges

FOR THE SLOW COOKER

Follow the chicken variation, right (shrimp will overcook in the slow cooker), reserving the fish sauce and soy sauce until the end. Cook on High for 2 hours or on Low for 4 hours, then stir in the fish sauce and soy sauce just before serving.

Absolutely everyone who has ever cooked this flavor-forward Thai-inspired dinner has said the same thing: "Fastest dinner ever!" I hope you know by now that fast doesn't have to mean bland or lackluster. Here, coconut milk and red curry paste work quick magic on shrimp (or chicken, tofu, or cauliflower, if that's more your style) faster than you can set the table.

1. Season the shrimp with the salt and pepper.

2. Put the coconut oil in the inner pot of the pressure cooker and set to Saute. Add the chile and ginger and cook until fragrant, about 1 minute. Add the curry paste (careful—it may splatter) and stir to brown slightly, about 1 minute. Add the coconut milk, soy sauce, and fish sauce (if using) and add the shrimp, stirring to coat.

3. Lock on the lid and Pressure Cook on high pressure for 1 minute. Release the pressure manually and open the lid.

4. Spoon the curry over warm jasmine rice and garnish with the herbs. Offer plenty of lime wedges for squeezing over the top.

TRY THIS! RED CURRY CHICKEN WITH BASIL AND LIME (GLUTEN-FREE)

Swap out the shrimp for 1¼ pounds boneless, skinless chicken breasts, cut into 1-inch pieces. Follow the recipe as instructed; if desired, add 1 small zucchini, cut into 1-inch pieces, along with the chicken. Lock on the lid and Pressure Cook on high pressure for 3 minutes instead of 1 minute.

Coconut Salmon
with Fresh Herbs and Lime

PREP TIME: 8 MINUTES
TOTAL TIME: 20 MINUTES
SERVES 4
GLUTEN-FREE DAIRY-FREE

4 center-cut salmon fillets (about 1½ pounds total), skin discarded and pin bones removed

1 teaspoon fine sea salt

¼ teaspoon freshly ground black pepper

2 tablespoons coconut oil or canola oil

1 fresh green chile, such as serrano or jalapeño, thinly sliced

1 (2-inch) piece fresh ginger, peeled and minced

1 (13.5-ounce) can unsweetened full-fat coconut milk

1 teaspoon fish sauce

1 teaspoon ground turmeric

1 to 2 tablespoons fresh lime juice

FOR SERVING

Cooked jasmine rice or other long-grain white rice

2 packed cups fresh basil, cilantro, or mint leaves, or a combination

Lime wedges

When my family moved from New York City to upstate New York, I craved the fast, flavorful takeout dinners we left behind. As I was wishing for more lightning fast, tasty meals, Kay Chun's Coconut Salmon Curry came across my radar, and I've been riffing on salmon and coconut ever since. Steam-poaching the fish in coconut milk keeps it moist and gives it instant flavor. For a full one-pot meal, toss in about 12 ounces sliced shiitake or snap peas (or as Kay does, add baby spinach) along with the fish.

1. Season the salmon with the salt and pepper.

2. Put the coconut oil, chile, and ginger in the inner pot of the pressure cooker and set to Saute. Cook until fragrant, about 1 minute.

3. Add the coconut milk, fish sauce, and turmeric. Lay in the seasoned salmon. Lock on the lid and Pressure Cook on high pressure for 1 minute for medium-rare or 2 minutes for well done. Release the pressure manually, open the lid, and stir in the lime juice.

4. Serve the fish with the broth over jasmine rice. Garnish with the herbs and serve with lime wedges for squeezing over the top.

COOK'S NOTE

Spicy Coconut Salmon: For a spicy kick, add 1 to 2 teaspoons Sriracha to the inner pot along with the coconut milk.

Mussels in White Wine
with Spaghetti

PREP TIME: 10 MINUTES
TOTAL TIME: 25 MINUTES
SERVES 4 TO 6
GLUTEN-FREE

4 tablespoons (½ stick) unsalted butter

1 small onion, finely chopped

4 garlic cloves, thinly sliced

2 sprigs fresh thyme, rosemary, or oregano

1 bay leaf

¼ teaspoon red pepper flakes

¼ teaspoon fine sea salt

2 pounds mussels, scrubbed and debearded

¾ cup dry white wine, such as Sauvignon Blanc

Juice of 1 lemon

FOR SERVING

Lemon wedges

Spaghetti or Perfect Toast (see box, page 48), optional
*For gluten-free, omit bread or use gluten-free bread

⅓ cup roughly chopped fresh parsley or cilantro

How do you like the sound of a seafood dinner that cooks in 2 minutes? That's how quickly a pressure cooker can get water boiling, and steam open a few pounds of beautiful mussels in a saturated, flavorful broth. Spend your time building flavor with garlic and bay leaf (and by "time" I mean a scant 2 minutes), and then let your pressure cooker do the rest. You can serve this over spaghetti, if you have the patience for the 8 whole minutes it takes to cook it on the stovetop, or just serve the mussels with broiled buttered bread (see Perfect Toast, page 48) for a quick, healthy meal. You can make this with clams, too, for an at-home *linguine alle vongole*.

1.   Place the butter in the inner pot of the pressure cooker and set to Saute. When the butter is melted, add the onion, garlic, herb sprigs, bay leaf, red pepper flakes, and salt and cook until the onion is slightly softened, 5 to 6 minutes.

2.   Add the mussels and wine, stirring to coat. Lock on the lid and Pressure Cook on high pressure for 2 minutes. Release the pressure manually, then open the lid. Check to make sure the mussels are all open; discard any that aren't. Discard the bay leaf and herb sprigs.

3.   Stir in the lemon juice. Serve over spaghetti or with toasted bread, sprinkle with parsley. Offer lemon wedges for squeezing.

TRY THIS! MUSSELS IN WHITE WINE AND TOMATO SAUCE

Add 1 minced small shallot and ½ cup finely chopped prosciutto along with the garlic. Add 1 (14.5-ounce) can of diced tomatoes along with the mussels and wine.

TRY THIS! SPICY CHORIZO CLAMS

Scrub 2 pounds littleneck clams. Add 1 minced small shallot, 1 cup fresh chorizo (squeezed from its casing), and an extra pinch of red pepper flakes when you add the garlic. Add 1 (14.5-ounce) can diced tomatoes and the clams along with the wine. Finish with a sprinkle of chopped fresh cilantro.

Saucy Chicken and Olives
with Greens

PREP TIME: 10 MINUTES
TOTAL TIME: 40 MINUTES,
(plus curing time)
SERVES 4
GLUTEN-FREE

2 pounds bone-in, skin-on chicken thighs or legs (see Cook's Note)

2 teaspoons fine sea salt

½ teaspoon freshly ground black pepper

Pinch of red pepper flakes

2 tablespoons extra-virgin olive oil

1 shallot or ½ small onion, thinly sliced

2 garlic cloves, thinly sliced

1 bunch kale or chard, ribs and stems removed, leaves roughly chopped (about 4 cups)

¾ cup chicken broth (such as on page 178) or store bought

2 teaspoons white wine vinegar

½ heaping cup meaty green olives, such as Castelvetrano, pitted or unpitted (see Cook's Note)

2 tablespoons unsalted butter

FOR SERVING

Creamy Parmesan Polenta (page 89), cooked rice, or buttered noodles

¼ cup fresh dill, parsley leaves, or a combination, roughly chopped

Flaky sea salt, such as Maldon

Chicken and olives, a French classic that never gets old, performs beautifully under pressure, yielding a tender chicken and plump, juicy olives with an instant sauce. If you can plan ahead, give the chicken a quick dry cure by rubbing it with a mixture of salt, pepper, and red pepper flakes; do this up to 24 hours ahead of the cooking, and flavors of the dry brine will penetrate the chicken right down to the bone. Serve this over the cheesy polenta, with all the flavorful sauce from the pot.

1. Pat the chicken dry with paper towels and lay out on a paper towel-lined tray or plate. Mix the salt, pepper, and red pepper flakes in a small bowl and rub the mixture all over the chicken. Set the chicken aside to dry-cure at room temperature, uncovered, for 30 minutes, or cover loosely with film or foil and refrigerate overnight.

2. Add the olive oil to the inner pot of the pressure cooker and set to Saute. Add the chicken, skin side down, and cook until beginning to brown, 8 to 10 minutes; in batches if needed. (Don't bother flipping; only the skin side needs to render.) Add the shallot, garlic, kale, broth, vinegar, and olives.

3. Lock on the lid and Pressure Cook on high pressure for 10 minutes. Release the pressure manually. Open the lid and add the butter, swirling it to thicken the sauce slightly.

4. Serve the chicken on a bed of polenta. Spoon the saucy greens, olives, and juices over the top and sprinkle with the herbs and flaky salt.

COOK'S NOTE

What's with the Pits? I love cooking with whole, unpitted olives. But be sure to warn your crowd that the pits are there, especially if there are kids involved. If your crew doesn't care for the hassle, make this with pitted olives instead.

COOK'S NOTE

Leave the Skin On? Cooking skin-on chicken in a pressure cooker is a nice extra step, if you have the time. You can use the Saute function to brown the chicken, but once you seal the pot, know that the moisture inside prevents the chicken skin from staying crisp. It will still be deeply flavorful, however, with tender, juicy meat. If you want to make things even easier, opt for boneless, skinless pieces here, and skip the step of browning.

Moroccan Spiced Chicken and Rice

PREP TIME: 15 MINUTES
TOTAL TIME: 40 MINUTES
SERVES 4
GLUTEN-FREE

1½ cups long-grain white rice

Juice of 1 lemon

3 garlic cloves, thinly sliced

2 teaspoons ground cumin

2 teaspoons ground paprika

1 teaspoon ground turmeric

Fine sea salt and freshly ground black pepper

4 tablespoons extra-virgin olive oil

1½ pounds boneless, skinless chicken thighs (about 6 thighs)

1 medium onion, finely chopped

1½ cups chicken broth (such as on page 178)

1 cinnamon stick

⅓ cup raisins

FOR SERVING

Homemade Yogurt (page 160) or store-bought plain whole-milk yogurt

1 cup fresh parsley and mint leaves, torn or roughly chopped

1 lemon, cut into wedges

This one-pot meal is rich with warming aromas of spices often found in Moroccan cooking that will send your family rushing to the table. Tweak to your taste (not a raisin crowd? skip them), but don't hold back on the fresh herbs at the end. The key to a delicious all-in-one chicken-and-rice dish in a pressure cooker is making sure you don't overcook the rice or add too much liquid, which will yield mushy rice. It's hard to believe this whole thing cooks in just 4 to 6 minutes (once you've browned the onions), but trust me on this.

1. Soak the rice in water for 15 minutes (see Cook's Note, page 102). Meanwhile, in a medium bowl, combine the lemon juice, garlic, cumin, paprika, turmeric, 1 teaspoon salt, ½ teaspoon pepper, and 3 tablespoons of the olive oil. Add the chicken pieces and turn to coat. Set aside to marinate while the rice soaks.

2. Place the remaining tablespoon olive oil in the inner pot of the pressure cooker and set to Saute. When the oil is hot, add the onion and cook, stirring frequently, until slightly browned, 4 to 6 minutes.

3. Drain the rice and add it to the inner pot. Stir in the broth, cinnamon stick, and 1 teaspoon salt, then add the chicken and its marinade.

4. Lock on the lid and Pressure Cook on high pressure for 6 minutes. Release the pressure manually and open the lid. Discard the cinnamon stick. Stir in the raisins and leave on the Keep Warm setting until ready to serve.

5. Place the chicken on individual plates, top each with some yogurt, sprinkle with the herbs. Serve with lemon wedges on the side.

TRY THIS! CHICKEN PITAS WITH TAHINI YOGURT SAUCE

Make the recipe as instructed, but skip the rice. Also, reduce the broth to 1 cup when cooking the chicken. Then shred the cooked chicken and stuff it into warmed pitas along with some tomato and cucumber slices, shredded lettuce, and Tahini-Yogurt Sauce (see box, page 131).

Quick Pork Bolognese for a Crowd

PREP TIME: 15 MINUTES
TOTAL TIME: 1 HOUR 10 MINUTES
SERVES 6 TO 8

3 tablespoons extra-virgin olive oil

½ medium onion, finely chopped

1 celery stalk, finely chopped

1 large carrot, finely chopped

6 large garlic cloves, finely chopped

2 anchovies, finely chopped

1½ pounds ground pork

½ pound ground beef

⅓ cup tomato paste

1 tablespoon harissa or hot pepper paste (optional)

¾ cup dry red wine, such as Merlot

1 (28-ounce) can whole San Marzano or plum tomatoes

2 bay leaves

1 sprig fresh rosemary

2 teaspoons fine sea salt

1¼ teaspoons freshly ground black pepper, plus more to taste

FOR SERVING

1 pound pasta of choice, or Creamy Parmesan Polenta (page 89)

Fresh ricotta cheese or finely grated parmesan cheese

½ cup fresh mint or parsley leaves, torn or roughly chopped

As satisfying as a spaghetti-and-meatball dinner is, a quicker way to get that same satisfaction is to enjoy a big, bold Bolognese sauce over pasta (called *ragu allà Bolognese*, a meaty sauce that hails from Bologna). Bolognese sauce takes a quarter of the time to reach maximum flavor in a pressure cooker. Most Bolognese sauces use beef as the headliner, but my favorite blend is mostly pork, with a bit of ground beef (grass-fed, if you can find it) mixed in. Feel free to play around with the ratio as long as you don't skimp on the aromatics. To serve, I love a long noodle, like tagliatelle or pappardelle, but any pasta will work. Or try the sauce on top of Creamy Parmesan Polenta (page 89). Either way, a dollop of creamy ricotta and the surprise of fresh mint are welcome additions.

1. Pour the olive oil into the inner pot of the pressure cooker and set to Saute. When the oil is hot, add the onion, celery, carrot, garlic, and anchovies and cook until slightly softened, about 6 minutes. Add the pork and beef and cook, breaking them up with a wooden spoon, until browned, about 8 minutes.

2. Add the tomato paste and harissa (if using); cook, stirring, for 1 minute to lightly toast. Add the wine, stirring to release any browned bits from the bottom of the pot. Cook for 4 minutes to cook off the alcohol and reduce.

3. Crush the tomatoes with a potato masher in a bowl. Add the tomatoes and their juices, the bay leaves, rosemary, salt, and 1¼ teaspoons pepper to the pot. Lock on the lid and Pressure Cook on high pressure for 30 minutes. Release the steam manually. Open the lid. The sauce should be deeply flavorful. Discard the bay leaves and rosemary sprig. Replace the lid, but do not lock it on. Leave on the Keep Warm setting until ready to serve.

4. When ready to serve, cook the pasta in boiling salted water until al dente. Drain and spoon the sauce over the pasta. Top with fresh ricotta or grated parmesan, a sprinkle of the fresh herbs, and more black pepper to taste.

COOK'S NOTE

Heat It Up: For a spicier Bolognese, double the harissa, or use Hungarian hot pepper paste and stir it in with the tomato paste.

Sauce with Depth of Flavor: A traditional Bolognese sauce cooks for hours on the stovetop. To mimic the depth and complexity of flavors you get from long cooking, I add both anchovy (for umami, or depth) and harissa (for spicy heat), which are excellent pantry staples that will serve you well in this recipe and others.

TRY THIS!: WILD MUSHROOM BOLOGNESE
(VEGAN VEGETARIAN)

Replace the pork and beef with 2¼ pounds finely chopped mixed mushrooms (cremini, button, maitake, shiitake, or oyster; a food processor makes quick work of the mushrooms) plus a splash of soy sauce. Use as many different types of mushrooms as you can. Buttons are juicy, while maitake, shiitake, and oysters lend incredible depth and meatiness. Follow the recipe as instructed, but after pressure cooking, release the pressure manually, open the lid, and cook on the Saute setting for 10 minutes to thicken the sauce. (Mushrooms release a lot of water, and cooking them further will deepen the sauce's flavor.)

Pulled Pork Tacos

PREP TIME: 20 MINUTES
TOTAL TIME: 1½ HOURS
(includes curing time)
SERVES 4 TO 6
GLUTEN-FREE

1 (3- to 4-pound) boneless Boston butt or pork shoulder roast, cut into 4 equal pieces

1 tablespoon fine sea salt

2 teaspoons freshly ground black pepper

1 teaspoon hot, smoked, or sweet paprika

3 garlic cloves, chopped

3 tablespoons soy sauce or tamari (gluten-free soy sauce)

2 tablespoons coconut sugar or dark brown sugar

2 tablespoons rice vinegar

1 tablespoon toasted sesame oil

1 cup beer of choice

FOR SERVING

12 corn tortillas, warmed

2 firm-ripe avocados, peeled and sliced

1 green chile, such as jalapeño or serrano, seeded and thinly sliced

Fresh cilantro leaves

4 small or 2 large radishes, thinly sliced

Pico de Gallo (see page 131) or fresh salsa

We don't cook a big hunk of meat all that often in our semi-vegetarian household (half of us eat meat, half of us don't), but when we do, we make it count. Pulled pork fits the bill—a juicy, flavorful feast that is easily shredded to be stuffed into sweet potatoes (see page 109) or used to top a morning congee (see page 36). It can also be sprinkled over nachos or, as here, rolled in warm tortillas and served with all your favorite taco fixings. Here I step away from Mexican tradition and add soy sauce to the marinade for its instant depth. Bonus: this cooked pork stores like a dream. It holds its flavor under a layer of fat in the freezer for months and is always on hand for instant family meals. Don't be afraid of the soy sauce here; it just adds depth of flavor.

1. Season the pork with the salt, pepper, and paprika. Leave at room temperature for 30 minutes.

2. Whisk together the garlic, soy sauce, sugar, vinegar, and sesame oil in the inner pot of the pressure cooker. Add the pork, turning to coat well, then pour the beer over everything.

3. Lock on the lid and Pressure Cook on high pressure for 1 hour. Let the pressure release naturally (up to 40 minutes); the pork will only get more tender as it sits. Open the lid and check the pork; it should be falling-apart tender.

4. Use two forks to shred the meat into bite-size pieces. Fill warm tortillas with the pork, then top with the avocado, chile, cilantro, radishes, and pico de gallo.

FOR THE SLOW COOKER

Prepare the pork as instructed through step 2, but in the slow cooker. Close and cook on High for 6 hours or Low for 8 to 10 hours, until the meat is falling apart and shreds easily. Then shred the meat and make the tacos as instructed.

COOK'S NOTE

Give It a Kick: If you love your pulled pork spicy, add up to 2 tablespoons Tabasco sauce or hot pepper paste (I love Hungarian paprika paste) to the pot along with the beer.

Simple Saag Paneer

PREP TIME: 15 MINUTES
TOTAL TIME: 25 MINUTES
SERVES 4
GLUTEN-FREE VEGETARIAN

1 tablespoon ghee (clarified butter; see Cook's Note, page 66) or unsalted butter, plus more if desired

1 small onion, finely chopped

1 tablespoon minced peeled fresh ginger

3 garlic cloves, roughly chopped

1 green chile, such as serrano or jalapeño, seeded and roughly chopped

1½ teaspoons ground coriander

1 teaspoon cumin seeds

1 teaspoon garam masala

¼ teaspoon ground turmeric

½ cup water, plus more as needed

16 ounces greens (spinach, baby kale, chard, mustard), tough stems and ribs removed

1 teaspoon fine sea salt

8 ounces paneer (Indian cheese; see Cook's Note)

FOR SERVING

Biryani Rice (page 101), optional

Homemade Yogurt (page 162) or store-bought plain yogurt or Cucumber Raita (see page 131)

This northern Indian dish of cheese (*paneer*) stewed in spinach gravy is traditionally made with any combination of leafy greens, including spinach, mustard, collard, or fenugreek. If you have a garden or a weekly CSA box, this recipe offers a way of using your abundance of greens that's satisfying and rich but still vegetable-forward. This is a great introduction to Indian food, too. Serve this with naan or basmati rice for a deeply satisfying, simple one-pot meal.

1.   Place the ghee in the inner pot of the pressure cooker and set to Saute. Add the onion, ginger, garlic, and chile and cook until the onion is soft, 4 to 5 minutes. Stir in the coriander, cumin, garam masala, and turmeric and stir constantly for 1 minute to toast the spices.

2.   Add ½ cup water, greens, and salt to the inner pot. Lock on the lid and Pressure Cook on high pressure for 0 minutes, just to steam the greens. (Yes, set the timer to 0—you just want to build up pressure without the greens overcooking and turning brown.) Release the pressure manually.

3.   Open the lid and let the greens cool for 5 minutes. Puree the greens with an immersion blender until smooth (adding a few tablespoons water, if needed, to get things moving; if you have an 8-quart pressure cooker, you may need to transfer the greens to an upright blender).

4.   Set the pressure cooker to Saute again and add the paneer and 1 teaspoon butter (if using). Heat until the cheese is warm and tender, about 1 minute.

5.   Serve warm with naan and yogurt.

FOR THE SLOW COOKER Omit the onion and add everything but the paneer to the pot. Cook on High for 2 hours. Puree the greens with an immersion blender. Stir in the paneer and cook on High for 1 hour more.

COOK'S NOTE **Herb Paneer:** If you want to change the flavor, swap in some mint, parsley, or dill for part of the greens (still totaling 16 ounces)

COOK'S NOTE **No Paneer? No Problem:** If you can't find paneer, sub in queso fresco (Mexican-style fresh cheese) or even firm tofu (not a cheese but a great protein sub for vegans); other firm cheeses, like halloumi, will also work but will be saltier, so reduce the salt.

Double-the-Vegetables Pot Roast

PREP TIME: 20 MINUTES
TOTAL TIME: 1½ HOURS
(includes curing time)
SERVES 4 TO 6
GLUTEN-FREE

1 (2½- to 3-pound) boneless beef chuck roast or brisket, trimmed of excess fat

1¼ teaspoons fine sea salt, plus more to taste

Freshly ground black pepper

1 tablespoon extra-virgin olive oil

1 large onion, thinly sliced

3 celery stalks, cut into 1-inch pieces

2 garlic cloves, thinly sliced

1 tablespoon harissa paste or tomato paste (see Cook's Note on page 130)

1 bay leaf

1 tablespoon all-purpose flour or gluten-free flour

½ cup dry white wine, such as Sauvignon Blanc

5 large carrots, cut into 1-inch pieces

2 cups beef or chicken broth (such as on pages 176, 178)

6 baby potatoes (white or red), halved

4 whole canned San Marzano tomatoes, drained and cut into 1-inch pieces

1 tablespoon apple cider vinegar (optional)

FOR SERVING

1 packed cup fresh mint leaves, dill leaves, or a combination, roughly chopped

Flaky sea salt, such as Maldon

Freshly ground black pepper

When I was growing up, pot roast was one of my favorite meals. While there was always plenty of meat and *jus*, it always felt like we were splitting two carrots six ways. I wanted *all* the carrots, and then some, so my grown-up pot roast has an abundance of them—plus little red or white potatoes that cook to a creamy finish in the pressure cooker. Normally this meal would take 2½ hours to prepare, but using a pressure cooker shaves down the time to under an hour! Feel free to load this up with all the veggies *you* love, and when it's cooked, sop up the juices with buttered bread. And don't skimp on the flaky salt and tons of fresh herbs at the finish (meat stewed in broth, though spoon-tender, usually needs that pop of herbs and seasoning to really shine). This dish is even better reheated, so even if you're a small family, don't let the quantity scare you off. You'll be meals ahead.

1. Season the roast on all sides with 1 teaspoon of the salt and some pepper and leave at room temperature for at least 30 minutes.

2. Pour the olive oil into the inner pot of the pressure cooker and set it to Saute. When the oil is hot, add the roast and brown on all sides, about 8 minutes total. Transfer to a plate.

3. Add the onion and celery to the inner pot, and cook, stirring often, until the onion has softened slightly, 5 to 7 minutes. Add the garlic, harissa, and bay leaf and cook until fragrant, 1 minute more. Sprinkle the flour over all and stir briskly for 30 seconds to coat. Add the wine and stir, about 1 minute.

4. Return the roast to the inner pot and add the carrots, broth, and the remaining ¼ teaspoon salt. Lock on the lid and Pressure Cook on high pressure for 45 minutes. Release the pressure manually.

5. Open the lid and add the potatoes and tomatoes to the inner pot. Lock on the lid again and Pressure Cook for 4 minutes on high pressure. Release the pressure manually and open the lid. The potatoes and beef should be tender but hold their shape.

(recipe continues)

In a skillet, brown the roast in the oil until it is a deep brown on two sides, about 10 minutes. Add all the remaining ingredients and the meat to a slow cooker and cook on High for 4 hours or Low for 6 to 8 hours. Then continue with the recipe instructions.

That Something Extra: The hint of harissa here, for heat and flavor, is subtle. It doesn't penetrate the meat, but it does give the *jus* just a little extra something. But if you have kids who are sensitive to spice, you can use simple tomato paste instead.

6. Taste and adjust the seasoning, adding more salt and pepper as needed and a splash of vinegar, if desired. Transfer the roast to a cutting board and let it rest for 10 to 15 minutes (to keep the roast juicy).

7. Meanwhile, cook the juices (with the vegetables) in the inner pot on the Saute setting until they thicken slightly, about 3 minutes. Leave on the Keep Warm setting until ready to serve.

8. Thinly slice the roast across the grain. Serve warm, with a generous quantity of vegetables, pouring the juices over the top. Top generously with the fresh herbs and sprinkle each portion with some flaky sea salt and freshly ground pepper.

TRY THIS! SHORT RIB SUPPER
(GLUTEN-FREE)

For an elegant bone-in beef dinner, replace the beef chuck with 3 pounds short ribs, preferably Korean or flanken style (cut across the bone). Follow the instructions, but skim any excess fat from the juices after cooking. Serve the short ribs warm over Creamy Parmesan Polenta (page 89), with plenty of fresh herbs or with the Shaggy Parmesan Gremolata (see box, page 75).

Three Easy Sauces

All the main courses in this chapter are *plenty* flavorful on their own, but if you're a dollop-and-dress-up kind of family (we are), you may occasionally crave a special sauce to serve on the side. These three (which double as dips) come together while your pressure cooker is doing the hard work, or they can be made ahead and kept at the ready for topping your family meals on the spot.

CUCUMBER RAITA

GLUTEN-FREE VEGETARIAN

This Indian-inspired yogurt dip adds a clean, cooling element when served alongside Chicken Tikka Masala (page 111), Chicken Biryani (see variation, page 101), or Simple Saag Paneer (page 126).

TO MAKE IT: Toast ½ teaspoon cumin seeds and 1 teaspoon brown mustard seeds in a small skillet on the stovetop, about 1 minute. Let cool, then grind in a coffee grinder or finely chop. Combine the toasted spices with 3 grated and squeezed-dry Persian cucumbers, 3 cups plain full-fat Greek yogurt, 1 tablespoon fresh lemon juice, 1 grated garlic clove, ⅓ cup chopped fresh cilantro or parsley, ¼ teaspoon fine sea salt, and a pinch of paprika. Stir, but don't overmix—leave some streaks. Serve sprinkled with more paprika and herbs and drizzle with olive oil, if desired.

TAHINI-YOGURT SAUCE

GLUTEN-FREE VEGETARIAN

This heavy hitter, which takes cues from Middle Eastern street food, is a treat to dollop over One-Pot Moroccan Chicken and Rice (page 123), Stuffed Sweet Potato "Tacos" (page 109), or an impromptu salad made with soft-boiled eggs (see page 39), Marinated Picnic Beans (page 84), mixed greens, and chopped cucumbers.

TO MAKE IT: Loosely stir together 1 cup plain whole-milk regular or Greek yogurt, 2 tablespoons fresh lime juice, 1 tablespoon tahini paste, 3 grated garlic cloves, ¼ cup chopped dill, 2 tablespoons chopped fresh mint, and ¼ teaspoon fine sea salt. Thin with up to 1 tablespoon water, if desired. Serve sprinkled with more dill and drizzled with olive oil, if desired.

PICO DE GALLO

GLUTEN-FREE DAIRY-FREE
VEGAN VEGETARIAN

Taco night isn't the same without pico de gallo—a fresh and chunky Mexican salsa made from chopped tomatoes, onions, green chiles, and cilantro. Use this to top Pulled Pork Tacos (page 125) or to stuff into burritos with cheese, avocado, and juicy shredded chicken. Keep it on hand for Stuffed Sweet Potato "Tacos" night (see page 109) and for Refried Beans (page 98).

TO MAKE IT: Chop 2 ripe, flavorful tomatoes, such as an heirloom variety. Stir together the tomatoes, ¼ medium finely chopped onion, 2 finely chopped seeded jalapeños, ⅓ cup chopped cilantro, 3 tablespoons lime juice, and ¼ teaspoon fine sea salt. Let sit, uncovered, for about 10 minutes before serving.

SIMPLE
DESSERTS

Even in a healthy family diet, there's still room for dessert. The good news is that a pressure cooker shines at making simple sweets that are (mostly) pretty good for you. My family does not need more cakes, cookies, and pies that are loaded with sugar and take hours to make—and I bet yours doesn't either. What we *do* need more of is yummy stewed fruit that tastes like heaven on its own and that blows your mind when spooned over ice cream, or an almost-instant berry crumble (see page 142) that radiates summer bliss, or a no-fail creamy chocolate pudding (see page 137), or a stunning caramel flan (see page 138). You'll find them all here. Meet six simple desserts (plus two decadent special-occasion cakes) that are easy enough to throw together on a weeknight and adaptable enough to dress up for guests.

Stewed Cinnamon Plums

PREP TIME: 5 MINUTES
TOTAL TIME: 20 MINUTES
SERVES 4 TO 6
GLUTEN-FREE DAIRY-FREE
VEGAN VEGETARIAN

8 large purple plums (about 2½ pounds), halved and pitted

2 teaspoons coconut oil or extra-virgin olive oil

2 to 3 tablespoons pure maple syrup

1 vanilla bean, split, or 1 teaspoon vanilla extract

1 cinnamon stick

¼ cup water

FOR THE SLOW COOKER

Add all the ingredients to the slow cooker and cook until the plums are juicy and tender, 2½ hours on High or 4 hours on Low.

Few things are more alluring than a saucy bowl of stewed fruit, perfect for spooning over pancakes, yogurt, or everyone's favorite, ice cream. Many stone fruits can be stewed in a pressure cooker with great success, but for me, it's plums that take the cake. They're deeply hued, easy to pit, and don't require peeling (their skins are paper-thin, especially when cooked). Plus, they are transformed into an instant-luxe sauce under pressure. Adjust the amount of maple syrup to match your sweet tooth or the season (ripe summer fruit needs less sweetening; off-peak fruit needs more).

1. Combine the plums, oil, 2 tablespoons maple syrup, vanilla, cinnamon stick, and water in the inner pot of the pressure cooker. Lock on the lid and Pressure Cook on high pressure for 2 minutes (if the plums are really ripe and juicy) to 4 minutes (for very firm plums).

2. Let the pressure release naturally (about 10 minutes) or release it manually. Open the lid and discard the cinnamon stick. Let the plums cool slightly.

3. Taste the plums and add the remaining tablespoon maple syrup to sweeten, if needed. Serve warm, or cool completely and refrigerate in an airtight container for up to 1 week.

TRY THIS! LEMON VERBENA
POACHED PEACHES OR APRICOTS
(GLUTEN-FREE DAIRY-FREE VEGAN VEGETARIAN)

I love the subtle, mysterious taste of the tender lemon verbena leaves that grow in my garden every summer, but you can use mint, thyme, or just about any other delicate-leaved herb you love. Replace the plums with peaches or apricots or use a mixture of both. Replace the cinnamon stick with a sprig of lemon verbena or mint and add ½ lemon to the pot.

Deep Dark Chocolate Pudding

PREP TIME: 10 MINUTES
TOTAL TIME: 3 HOURS
(includes chilling time)
SERVES 4 TO 6
GLUTEN-FREE VEGETARIAN

6 ounces bittersweet chocolate, chopped

1 cup whole milk

1 cup half-and-half

5 large egg yolks

⅓ packed cup light or dark brown sugar or coconut sugar

2 teaspoons vanilla extract

Pinch of fine sea salt

EQUIPMENT: 6 by 3-inch or 7 by 3-inch ceramic ramekin

We're a pudding family. I'm *so* not bothered by whipping up a from-scratch pudding on the stovetop, because it's always worth it, and we almost always have the ingredients to pull it off: milk, eggs, chocolate, sugar. Still, a hands-off version (i.e., no stirring)—a true set-it-and-forget-it from-scratch pudding—is another of life's little gifts, and one I'll gladly accept. I suggest you do, too.

I've learned that cooking this pudding on low pressure yields a looser, creamier pudding, while high pressure produces a soufflé-meets-mousse texture that my family finds irresistible. Either way, it's a little miracle that I can get behind. Let the pudding cool completely before serving or even dipping in. To get the right texture, it's essential that the steam settles. Dive in too early, and you'll upset the delicate balance and flawless presentation.

1. Place the chocolate in a medium metal bowl. Combine the milk and half-and-half in a medium saucepan (or a bowl in the microwave) and bring to a simmer over medium-low heat. Pour the milk over the chocolate, and whisk until melted and smooth.

2. Whisk together the egg yolks, brown sugar, vanilla, and salt in a medium bowl until completely smooth. Gradually pour the hot chocolate mixture into the yolks, starting with 1 cup (so the eggs don't cook), and then adding the remaining chocolate mixture, whisking constantly to combine. (You can pause and store this mixture for up to 2 days in the fridge.)

3. Pour the chocolate custard into the ramekin and cover tightly with foil. Pour about 1½ cups water into the inner pot of the pressure cooker. Set the ramekin on a steamer rack or trivet and use the handles to carefully lower it into the water, taking care not to splash any into the dish. Lock on the lid and Pressure Cook on low pressure (for a creamier finish) or high pressure (for a mousse-like finish) for 18 minutes. Let the steam release naturally (about 20 minutes).

4. Open the lid and lift the ramekin out of the pot. Remove the foil, cool to room temperature, and chill for 2 to 3 hours, or until ready to serve. The pudding will keep, covered and refrigerated, for up to 3 days.

Easy Caramel Flan

PREP TIME: 12 MINUTES
TOTAL TIME: 3 HOURS
SERVES 4 TO 6
GLUTEN-FREE VEGETARIAN

CARAMEL

½ cup granulated sugar

CUSTARD

1 cup half-and-half

1 cup whole milk

5 large eggs

⅓ cup granulated sugar

1 teaspoon pure vanilla extract

Pinch of fine sea salt

EQUIPMENT: 6 by 3-inch or
  7 by 3-inch ceramic ramekin or
  round metal cake pan

FOR THE SLOW COOKER

Mix the ingredients as instructed and pour into a 6-inch ramekin. Place the ramekin, well wrapped, on a trivet in the slow cooker along with the 1½ cups water. Cook on High for 2½ hours. Remove the ramekin from the cooker, then chill and serve.

COOK'S NOTE

Quick Caramel: Yes, you can skip the first step and use store-bought caramel for this, but look for a product without any additives. You need real caramelized sugar to give a clean release and a glassy finish to the cooked flan, so ingredients should read something like: "sugar and butter"—that is, no fake flavors or fillers.

Flan—a classic Spanish custard—is the kind of fancy*ish* dessert that seems harder than it is. To make it, you line a pan with homemade caramel, then whip up a simple, luscious vanilla custard (made of eggs and milk) to pour over the top. The whole thing is baked in one pan, then flipped onto a plate, where the caramel flows down the pudding like lava, yielding restaurant-level elegance with home-cooked ease. This is a recipe that works beautifully in the pressure cooker, requiring only a little patience for the necessary 3-hour chill. And it will all be worth it—so very worth it.

1. Heat ½ cup sugar in a small, straight-sided saucepan over medium-low heat. Cook without stirring (which can disrupt caramelization) until the sugar has melted and browned into a golden caramel, 4 to 7 minutes. After the sugar has melted, swirl gently to incorporate any parts that are browning faster than others. Pour the warm caramel into the ramekin, swirling to coat the bottom.

2. Whisk together the half-and-half, milk, eggs, remaining ⅓ cup sugar, vanilla, and salt in a medium bowl. (I like to blitz this mixture with an immersion blender or in an upright blender to make sure it's perfectly smooth.) Gently pour the custard over the caramel layer, taking care not to disturb the caramel.

3. Pour about 1½ cups water into the inner pot of the pressure cooker. Cover the ramekin tightly with foil, then set it on a steamer rack or trivet, and lower it into the inner pot.

4. Lock on the lid and Pressure Cook on low pressure for 18 minutes. Let the pressure release naturally (about 20 minutes).

5. Open the lid and carefully lift the ramekin from the pot. Remove the foil and let the flan cool to room temperature. Chill until ready to serve, at least 2½ hours.

6. To serve, run a knife around the edge of the ramekin to loosen the flan. Place a plate on top and carefully flip it over, making sure the caramel doesn't spill. The flan will keep in the refrigerator, covered, for up to 2 days.

Vanilla and Cardamom Poached Pears

PREP TIME: 10 MINUTES
TOTAL TIME: 40 MINUTES
SERVES 8
GLUTEN-FREE DAIRY-FREE*
VEGAN* VEGETARIAN

8 small ripe pears (Anjou, Comice, Bartlett, or Williams), peeled

3 tablespoons pure maple syrup

1 vanilla bean, split, or 1 teaspoon vanilla extract

2 or 3 cardamom pods, crushed slightly

1 cinnamon stick

1 large strip of orange or lemon zest

½ cup water

Ice cream of choice or freshly whipped cream, for serving
  *Dairy-free and vegan with dairy-free ice cream

FOR THE SLOW COOKER

Cook the ingredients on Low until the pears are fork-tender, 4 to 5 hours (more time means deeper flavors and more tender pears).

Few things offer more easy elegance than whole poached pears. It's a trick I left behind at culinary school and had nearly forgotten—until the day I came home with a bag of beautiful but rock-hard red pears and didn't have the patience to let them ripen in a brown bag all week. I poached them to serve over scoops of our favorite vanilla ice cream, a great reminder that sometimes the best dessert can be the simplest one. Any leftovers are a welcome addition to tomorrow's breakfast, served over yogurt or porridge.

1. Leaving the stems intact, use a teaspoon to cut out the cores from the bottom of the pears. Set the pears upright in the inner pot of the pressure cooker.

2. Add the maple syrup, vanilla, cardamom pods, cinnamon stick, citrus zest, and water to the pot. Lock on the lid and Pressure Cook on high pressure for 10 minutes. Let the pressure release naturally (about 30 minutes). Open the lid and discard the cinnamon stick.

3. Serve the pears warm or at room temperature, with ice cream or whipped cream, with the juices poured over the top. Or let cool completely and refrigerate in an airtight container for up to 1 week.

Salted Dulce de Leche

PREP TIME: 5 MINUTES
TOTAL TIME: 1 HOUR 15 MINUTES
SERVES 4 TO 6
GLUTEN-FREE VEGETARIAN

½ teaspoon baking soda

3 tablespoons warm water

1 (14-ounce) can sweetened condensed milk

Flaky sea salt, such as Maldon (optional)

EQUIPMENT: 6- or 7-inch stainless-steel bowl

The promise of perfectly golden dulce de leche—a dreamy caramel-like confection—ready for pouring over sundaes, drizzling over hot chocolate, or dipping crisp fall apple slices into, is far too good to resist. Even if you've never made a dessert from scratch, you can do this. While you can make dulce de leche by heating an unopened can of sweetened condensed milk (either on the stovetop or in the pressure cooker), as people throughout Latin America have been doing for decades, I prefer this method, which is foolproof and worry-free.

1. Combine the baking soda and warm water in a small bowl, and stir to dissolve.

2. Pour the condensed milk and the baking soda mixture into the mixing bowl.

3. Pour about 1 cup cold water into the inner pot of the pressure cooker and place the mixing bowl in the pot. Lock on the lid and Pressure Cook on high pressure for 1 hour. Let the pressure release naturally (about 20 minutes). Open the lid. The mixture should be a rich golden brown, not too dark. If needed, lock on the lid again and Pressure Cook on high pressure for another 10 to 20 minutes (different brands of condensed milk can yield different cook times).

4. Carefully remove the bowl from the pressure cooker and stir vigorously with a whisk or immersion blender until smooth. Top with flaky sea salt, if desired, and serve warm or at room temperature.

Summer Berry Crumble

PREP TIME: 20 MINUTES
TOTAL TIME: 1 HOUR
SERVES 6
GLUTEN-FREE DAIRY-FREE
VEGAN VEGETARIAN

Nonstick cooking spray or
unsalted butter

4 cups mixed fresh berries,
such as hulled and halved
strawberries, blackberries,
raspberries, blueberries, or
even pitted cherries

2 tablespoons sugar

1 tablespoon cornstarch or
potato starch

1 cup old-fashioned rolled oats

⅓ cup almond flour

3 tablespoons pure maple syrup

1 teaspoon ground cinnamon

¼ teaspoon fine sea salt

4 tablespoons (½ stick) unsalted
butter, melted, or olive oil, or
coconut oil, melted

⅓ cup toasted sliced almonds,
or roughly chopped whole
almonds, walnuts, or hazelnuts
(see page 143)

FOR SERVING

Ice cream of choice

EQUIPMENT: 6 by 3-inch or
7 by 3-inch ceramic ramekin or
round metal cake pan

When I'm looking for a simple sweet on a hot summer day, one that can be made without turning on the oven (hello, the entire month of July!), this one does the trick. In a pressure cooker, the fresh berries collapse into juicy perfection in just 10 minutes.

The oat topping isn't as crispy-crunchy as you'd get in the oven, but I can live without a perfect crisp for all the pleasure this quick, healthy crumble brings. If you crave a crunchier topping, go heavy with the toasted nuts on top.

I love that this recipe makes enough for a family of four to six, served alongside ice cream, with just enough left over for breakfast the next day. We've been known to spoon this, warm or cold, over bowls of creamy yogurt for a not-too-sweet treat that's a nice alternative to muesli or cold cereal on quick mornings.

1. Spray the ramekin with cooking spray.

2. Toss the berries with the sugar and cornstarch in a bowl, then place in the prepared ramekin.

3. Mix the oats, almond flour, maple syrup, cinnamon, and salt in a bowl. Add the melted butter and stir to coat well. Sprinkle the mixture over the berries. Cover the ramekin tightly with foil, bringing the foil down the sides.

4. Pour about ¾ cup water into the inner pot of the pressure cooker. Set the ramekin on a trivet and carefully lower the trivet into the inner pot, taking care not to splash any water into the dish. Lock on the lid and Pressure Cook on high pressure for 10 minutes. Let the pressure release naturally (about 15 minutes).

5. Open the lid and carefully lift out the ramekin using the trivet's handles (they may be hot). Remove the foil and sprinkle the top with the toasted nuts. Serve warm, topped with a scoop of ice cream, if desired.

TOASTY TOPS

The pressure cooker is a moist environment, making a crisp topping an impossibility. To mimic the crisp oven finish, I toast nuts in bulk in advance and keep them in jars for sprinkling over yogurt bowls, salads, and this simple summer dessert. Here's how:

Preheat the oven to 350°F. Toss 2 cups whole almonds, walnuts, hazelnuts, or pecans with 2 tablespoons olive oil. Spread in an even layer on a baking sheet and toast until fragrant and golden, 6 to 8 minutes, stirring halfway through. Cool completely before storing in glass jars at room temperature for up to 1 month or in the fridge for 2 months. (For toasting sliced almonds, lower the baking time to 5 minutes total.)

Double Chocolate Cheesecake

PREP TIME: 35 MINUTES
TOTAL TIME: 5½ HOURS
(includes chilling)
SERVES 8
VEGETARIAN

Nonstick cooking spray

20 chocolate wafer cookies, or 10 full-size chocolate graham crackers

⅔ cup plus 1 tablespoon coconut sugar or dark brown sugar

4 tablespoons (½ stick) unsalted butter or coconut oil, melted

¾ teaspoon fine sea salt

2 (8-ounce) packages cream cheese, at room temperature

¼ cup heavy cream

1 tablespoon cornstarch

4 ounces bittersweet chocolate, melted

2 teaspoons vanilla extract

2 large eggs

Cocoa powder, for serving

EQUIPMENT: 6 by 3-inch or 7 by 3-inch round metal cake pan with a removable bottom, or 7-inch springform pan (see Cook's Note)

COOK'S NOTE

Preventing a Leaky Pan: You can avoid the paper-towel and foil wrapping by using a solid 6 by 3 or 7 by 3-inch cake pan without a springform or removable bottom. The solid pan will keep the crust and cake from absorbing any water while it cooks. Yes, it will make it harder to cut and serve the cheesecake, but after the first slice it's easier to cut into tidy pieces.

Cheesecake is a rich, decadent special-occasion food. Is it healthy? Not so much. But a small slice on occasion can't hurt, especially when it's homemade. The thing is, a pressure cooker is just *too good* at pulling off this treat, with minimal error (moist, creamy, no cracking), to pass up the opportunity. This double-chocolate version will delight the chocolate set, but if caramel or coffee is more your style, read on for that tweak. Citrus lovers, skip to page 147 for your dream cheesecake.

While you can turn out a perfect cheesecake with a pressure cooker fairly easily, you do need to mind the timing and visual clues. Don't be tempted to rush the process or to slice the cheesecake before it has fully chilled.

1. Coat the cake pan with cooking spray. Lay an 8-inch square of paper towel on a 10-inch square of foil and wrap the base of the cake pan. The paper towel should lie between the bottom of the pan and the foil; it's there to absorb moisture and prevent the crust from getting soggy.

2. In the bowl of a food processor, grind the cookies and 1 tablespoon of the sugar until finely ground; you should have about 1½ cups crumbs. Add the melted butter and ¼ teaspoon of the salt and pulse until combined and the mixture has the texture of wet sand. Transfer the crumb crust to the prepared pan and press into the bottom in an even layer with a flat-bottomed glass or jar. Place in the freezer to chill while you make the filling.

3. Beat the cream cheese, cream, cornstarch, and the remaining ⅔ cup sugar and ½ teaspoon salt with an electric mixer until completely smooth and lump-free, 1 to 2 minutes. Add the melted chocolate and vanilla; stir to combine. Add the eggs, one at a time, and beat on low until smooth but not aerated, about 30 seconds per egg.

4. Pour the filling into the prepared crust and tap the pan on the counter to remove any bubbles; smooth the top with an offset spatula. Cover the pan tightly with foil.

(recipe continues)

5. Pour about 1 cup water into the inner pot of the pressure cooker. Place a trivet in the pot and set the pan on top. Lock on the lid and Pressure Cook on high pressure for 40 minutes. Let the pressure release naturally (about 25 minutes); don't rush the pressure release or the cheesecake will be undercooked.

6. Open the lid and carefully lift the pan out of the pot. Remove the foil, taking care not to let any condensation drip onto the cheesecake. Let cool on the counter for 1 hour; the center third of the cheesecake will still be wobbly but will set up when chilled. Refrigerate for at least 4 hours, until set. To serve, dust the cheesecake with the cocoa powder before slicing.

TRY THIS! PEANUT BUTTER AND CHOCOLATE CHEESECAKE

Replace the chocolate with ½ cup creamy peanut butter (not natural) and Pressure Cook on high pressure for 36 minutes.

TRY THIS! CHOCOLATE ESPRESSO CHEESECAKE

Omit the melted chocolate. Warm the cream and stir in 1 tablespoon instant espresso powder before adding it to the cream cheese. Pressure Cook on high pressure for 38 minutes.

TRY THIS! DULCE DE LECHE CHEESECAKE

Use ⅓ cup dulce de leche, either homemade (see page 141) or store-bought, in place of the melted chocolate. Reduce the sugar in the filling to ⅓ cup. Pressure Cook on high pressure for 40 minutes.

Double Citrus Cheesecake

PREP TIME: 30 MINUTES
TOTAL TIME: 5½ HOURS
(includes chilling)
SERVES 8
VEGETARIAN

Nonstick cooking spray

20 thin almond or ginger cookies, or 10 full-size graham crackers

4 tablespoons (½ stick) unsalted butter or coconut oil, melted

½ teaspoon fine sea salt

2 (8-ounce) packages cream cheese, at room temperature

2 tablespoons heavy cream

⅓ cup granulated sugar

1 tablespoon cornstarch

1 teaspoon vanilla extract

2 teaspoons finely grated lemon or lime zest

2 tablespoons fresh lemon juice

2 large eggs

FOR THE TOPPING

½ cup sour cream or crème fraîche

1 tablespoon confectioners' sugar

EQUIPMENT: 6 by 3-inch or 7 by 3-inch round metal cake pan with a removable bottom, or 7-inch springform pan (see Cook's Note, page 144)

If you love a deeply creamy dessert with a bright citrusy finish, you've come to the right page. This tangy, just-sweet-enough cheesecake is classic and easy to embellish with a sour cream glaze, a big pile of fresh berries, or thin slices of citrus, like blood orange and lemon. Even in a pressure cooker, a cheesecake doesn't make itself. There are a few steps here to get this out of the gate, but they're worth it.

1. Coat the cake pan with cooking spray. Lay an 8-inch square of paper towel on a 10-inch square of foil and use it to wrap the base of the cake pan. (The paper towel should sit between the bottom of the pan and the foil; it is there to absorb moisture and keep your crust from getting soggy.)

2. Process the cookies in a food processor until finely ground; you should have about 1½ cups crumbs. Pulse in the melted butter and ¼ teaspoon of the salt until the mixture has the texture of wet sand.

3. Transfer the crumb crust to the prepared pan and press into the bottom in an even layer with a flat-bottomed glass or jar. Place in the freezer to chill while you make the filling.

4. Beat the cream cheese, cream, sugar, cornstarch, and the remaining ¼ teaspoon salt with an electric mixer until smooth and lump-free, 1 to 2 minutes. Add the vanilla, lemon zest, and lemon juice. Add the eggs, one at a time, and beat on low until smooth but not aerated, about 30 seconds per egg.

5. Pour the filling into the prepared crust and tap on the counter to remove any bubbles; smooth the top with an offset spatula. Cover the pan tightly with foil.

6. Pour about 1 cup water into the inner pot of the pressure cooker. Place a trivet in the pot and set the cheesecake on top. Lock on the lid and Pressure Cook on high pressure for 38 minutes. Let the pressure release naturally (about 25 minutes); don't rush the release or the cheesecake will be undercooked.

(recipe continues)

7. Open the lid and carefully lift the pan out of the inner pot. Remove the foil, taking care not to let any condensation drip onto the cheesecake. Let cool on the counter for 1 hour (the center third of the cheesecake will still be wobbly but will set up as it chills), then refrigerate for at least 4 hours, or until set.

8. Meanwhile, stir together the sour cream and confectioners' sugar. Spoon over the cooled cheesecake and spread in an even layer.

TRY THIS! REALLY VANILLA CHEESECAKE

Replace the citrus zest with the seeds scraped from a vanilla bean.

A SMALL BUT MIGHTY PAN (OR DISH!)

Many pressure cooker cakes and other sweets call for a special pan. I didn't want to invest in a whole new line of bakeware just to fit into my pressure cooker, and I don't want to ask you to, either. What does fit into an 6- or 8-quart pressure cooker is a 6 or 7 by 3-inch ceramic ramekin (think: soufflé dish) or a metal cake pan of the same size—which you might already have at home or can easily find at stores or online. You can use and reuse these simple pans for all these recipes, as well as in your oven for recipes you already know and love.

For cheesecakes, you may want to invest in a 7 by 3-inch cake pan with a removable bottom, or a 7-inch springform pan (though it's not absolutely necessary). Just be sure the depth of the pan is at least 3 inches (not 2 inches), and it can hold at least 4 cups (1 quart)—enough for a whole pudding, cheesecake, or flan.

COZY

DRINKS

Warm drinks, like hot cocoa and steamy cider, are one of life's little gifts—soothing and delicious, something worth building rituals around, even in the midst of busy family life. They warm the soul and the bones, and sometimes even satisfy a sweet tooth when you're trying to avoid sugary treats for a bit. Here are my five favorites, easy to love and repeat. Making them in a pressure cooker ensures you can sit down to a steamy cup of something comforting and inviting any time of the day, without the worry of burning it on the stovetop. Consider it a multitasker's gift.

Your electric pressure cooker is also a brilliant place to keep a big batch of something warm and spiced waiting for guests when you're hosting family or friends. Leave the inner pot of your pressure cooker on the Keep Warm setting (for hours on end, without scorching or burning), and ladle out something steamy and delicious to order. Bonus: your kitchen (or wherever you plug in your pot) will smell great!

Instant Nut Milk

PREP TIME: 5 MINUTES
TOTAL TIME: 15 MINUTES
MAKES 5 CUPS
GLUTEN-FREE DAIRY-FREE
VEGAN VEGETARIAN

1 cup raw nuts of choice

3 cups water

Pinch of fine sea salt

1 tablespoon pure maple syrup,
  or to taste

1 scant teaspoon vanilla extract,
  or to taste (optional)

TRY THIS! DAIRY-FREE
CAFÉ AU LAIT
(GLUTEN-FREE DAIRY-FREE
VEGAN VEGETARIAN)

Combine ¾ cup warm prepared nut
milk, with 2 tablespoons hot espresso
or ⅓ cup warm, strong-brewed coffee.
Use a milk frother to froth before
serving warm.

I've been making nut milk for years, letting nuts soak overnight in cold water and blending them the next day. It's not hard, but it does require some forethought. If you're new to making nut milk, you've chosen the right time to begin: a pressure cooker can quickly render the nuts soft enough to blend into a frothy milk substitute, with no soaking time required.

Making nut milk from your favorite nuts ensures a creamy, pure product with no added stabilizers, gums, or sweeteners. Cashews, peanuts, and hazelnuts yield the richest, creamiest nut milks, while almonds, pistachios, and walnuts offer leaner versions. Just make sure the nuts are raw and unsalted, and organic if you want to go the extra mile.

1. Combine the nuts and 1 cup of the water in the inner pot of the pressure cooker. Lock on the lid and Pressure Cook on low pressure for 2 to 5 minutes, depending on the density of the nuts (hazelnuts and almonds take longer to steam than, say, cashews or pecans). Let the steam release naturally (about 10 minutes).

2. Open the lid and transfer the nuts and their cooking liquid along with the remaining 2 cups water and the salt to a high-speed upright blender. Blend on high until creamy and frothy, 2 to 3 minutes.

3. Strain the mixture if you prefer a thinner, more skimmed-milk feeling. Sweeten to taste with maple syrup and up 1 teaspoon of vanilla, if desired. Return the nut milk to the inner pot and leave on the Keep Warm setting if using for warm coffee drinks, or let cool completely and store in an airtight container in the refrigerator for up to 3 days.

TRY THIS! CASHEW CREAM
(GLUTEN-FREE DAIRY-FREE VEGAN VEGETARIAN)

I like to make cashew cream, a delicious vegan alternative for thickening. Prepare the nut milk as instructed, but use 1 cup water to 1 cup cashews, plus ⅛ teaspoon fine sea salt. Do not add the additional 2 cups water.

French Hot Chocolate

2 cups whole milk

1 cup half-and-half

1 cup water

2 to 3 tablespoons pure maple syrup

1 teaspoon cornstarch

5 ounces semisweet or bittersweet chocolate, chopped

Whipped cream and chocolate shavings or marshmallows, for serving

In just 5 short minutes, this mixture of chopped chocolate, milk, half-and-half, and maple syrup is transformed into a rich and super-satisfying treat—the kind you might find on the Champs-Élysées in Paris. That's my kind of hot chocolate. Sure, you can make hot cocoa on the stovetop, but the pressure cooker is safer and more kid-friendly (mine *love* helping with this easy task, and I don't worry about their getting burned from the hot stove). It's easy to double and triple this recipe and to keep it warm for a crowd of neighborhood kids after a hearty romp in the snow.

1.   Place the milk, half-and-half, water, maple syrup, and cornstarch in the inner pot of the pressure cooker and stir to combine. Add the chocolate and set to Saute, whisking occasionally, until thickened and evenly chocolaty, about 3 minutes.

2.   Give the hot cocoa a vigorous whisk (or use an immersion blender or a milk frother) to combine and whip into a bubbly, steamy cup. Leave on the Keep Warm setting until ready to serve. Then pour into mugs and top with whipped cream and chocolate shavings or marshmallows, if desired.

TRY THIS! OAT-MILK HOT CHOCOLATE (GLUTEN-FREE DAIRY-FREE VEGAN VEGETARIAN)

Substitute 4 cups oat milk for the half-and-half, water, and milk. Try this also with almond or cashew milk.

HOMEMADE WHIPPED CREAM
GLUTEN-FREE VEGETARIAN

Desserts and hot drinks, especially hot chocolate, are great topped with freshly whipped cream. Here's how:

Whip 1 cup best-quality heavy cream with 1 teaspoon sugar and a splash of vanilla extract in a metal bowl, using a whisk or an electric beater, until the cream just holds soft peaks.

Golden Milk (Turmeric) Latte

PREP TIME: 5 MINUTES
TOTAL TIME: 20 MINUTES
SERVES 2 TO 4
GLUTEN-FREE DAIRY-FREE
VEGAN VEGETARIAN

1 (13.5-ounce) can unsweetened full-fat coconut milk, or 1½ cups almond milk, or a blend

1¼ cups water

2 teaspoons ground turmeric

2 tablespoons grated peeled fresh ginger, or 1 teaspoon ground ginger

1 cinnamon stick

3 to 4 tablespoons pure maple syrup or honey

A warm morning beverage is a treat for everyone, especially the person getting up early to pack lunches and make breakfast magic happen (that's me—and maybe you, too!). I fell in love with golden milk, a westernized name for haldi doodh, when I was trying to kick my daily hot-cocoa habit one winter. I'm not a coffee drinker, so I'm always looking for a frothy and satisfying morning-ritual replacement. Made from your milk of choice—from cow's milk to coconut milk—haldi doodh is loaded with potent anti-inflammatory spices like ginger and turmeric. And when the morning is too rushed and breakfast feels skimpy, I love knowing there is warm nourishment in every cup.

1. Place the coconut milk, water, turmeric, ginger, and cinnamon stick in the inner pot of the pressure cooker and stir to combine. Lock on the lid and Pressure Cook on low pressure for 2 minutes. Release the steam manually and open the lid. Discard the cinnamon stick.

2. Stir the mixture vigorously. (Don't be alarmed if the coconut milk looks curdled; it just needs a good stir.) Sweeten with the maple syrup and leave on the Keep Warm setting until ready to serve. Froth with a milk frother or a immersion blender, or a quick whiz in an upright blender, before serving.

DOUBLE IT

All the drinks in this chapter can easily be doubled, tripled, or more, depending on the size of your pressure cooker. A 6- or 8-quart pressure cooker has plenty of room to make a batch big enough for a crowd of up to 30 guests.

WORTH A STIR

All the milk-based (dairy or nondairy) drinks in this chapter benefit from a vigorous whisking or a few spins around the inner pot with a milk frother, before use. For the ultimate warm, frothy beverage, use an immersion blender or an upright blender to froth your drinks before serving.

Homemade Chai Masala

PREP TIME: 10 MINUTES
TOTAL TIME: 1 HOUR
SERVES 6
GLUTEN-FREE VEGETARIAN

6 cups water

4 cinnamon sticks

5 cardamom pods, crushed

3 whole cloves

1 (2-inch) piece peeled fresh
    ginger, sliced into coins

1 teaspoon fennel seeds, crushed

4 high-quality black tea bags

FOR SERVING

Milk of choice

Honey or pure maple syrup

COOK'S NOTE

Chaga Cha: Adding chaga, a dried mushroom thought to have anti-inflammatory properties, to your chai adds earthiness and supports the immune system (and bonus: you can use the same piece several times). Add 1 large piece dried chaga mushroom (about ½ ounce) along with the tea bags and spices before pressure cooking.

Making chai masala from scratch is a ritual I love to share with family and friends because this Indian drink is both healthful and incredibly nourishing, filling you head to toe with warming spices on short days and long, cold nights. (In contrast, boxed chai mixes are filled with sweeteners and stabilizers.) Making chai masala in a pressure cooker gives you a big pot to dip into all day long—perfect for groups and gatherings. You can even chill and keep it in the fridge to reheat later in the week, or serve over ice in the summer with the milk of your choice. For the black tea bags, use something high quality that you already love for the best flavor.

1. Place the water, cinnamon sticks, cardamom pods, cloves, ginger, and fennel seeds in the inner pot of the pressure cooker and stir to combine. Lock on the lid and Pressure Cook on low pressure for 10 minutes. Release the pressure naturally (the longer the spices steep, the more deeply flavored your chai will be: I often leave it for several hours).

2. Open the lid, add the tea bags, stirring well to immerse them, and steep in the hot liquid for 3 to 5 minutes, depending on how dark you like your tea. Pour the chai through a strainer, then return it to the pressure cooker. Leave on the Keep Warm setting until ready to serve. Add milk and honey to taste (see variation that follows). Serve warm, or cool the chai (before adding milk) and refrigerate any extra in an airtight container for up to 2 weeks to use as a chai concentrate.

TRY THIS! MILKY CHAI LATTE

In my house, we love our chai masala lightly sweetened and served with just about any kind of milk—from cow's milk to almond, oat, cashew, hazelnut, or even coconut milk, and then frothed into a creamy, sustaining drink. If you want to make the whole batch milky (as traditional chai would be, in India), add equal parts milk and chai to the inner pot of the pressure cooker and set to Saute (to heat quickly) or the Keep Warm setting (to heat slowly). Sweeten with honey to taste (2 to 4 tablespoons honey for the whole batch). Use an immersion blender or milk frother to thicken the mix to a frothy finish. Finish with a sprinkle of cinnamon sugar and serve warm.

Spiced Cider

PREP TIME: 5 MINUTES
TOTAL TIME: 15 MINUTES
SERVES 6
GLUTEN-FREE DAIRY-FREE
VEGAN VEGETARIAN

8 cups (2 quarts) apple cider

½ orange, scrubbed and sliced in rounds

4 whole cloves

2 cinnamon sticks

1 vanilla bean, split

1 (2-inch) piece of peeled fresh ginger, cut into coins (optional)

1 tart apple, such as a Crispin, Jonagold, Granny Smith, or Honeycrisp, cored and sliced

COOK'S NOTE

Ice It: Once you have strained the apple cider, you have a spiced-cider concentrate that is wonderful chilled and served over ice with a wedge of lemon in the summer. Cool the concentrate completely and refrigerate for up to 2 weeks.

Come fall, there's a string of birthday parties, apple-picking fêtes, and bonfires held by our friends that stretches right through Thanksgiving. We can always count on big pots of mulled cider at every party to satisfy small bellies during breezy outdoor days. It's easy to whip up and serve a crowd, and it makes the little ones feel as if they've had that *special* drink. Swap this out for the Mulled Wine variation that follows for the grown-up set.

1. Add 7 cups of the cider, the orange slices, cloves, cinnamon sticks, vanilla bean, and ginger (if using) to the inner pot of the pressure cooker and stir to combine. Lock on the lid and Pressure Cook on low pressure for 3 minutes. Release the steam manually and open the lid.

2. Pour the cider through a strainer and return it to the inner pot (see Cook's Note), adding the apple slices and the remaining 1 cup cider. Leave on the Keep Warm setting until ready to serve.

3. Ladle into mugs and garnish with the apple slices.

TRY THIS! MULLED WINE

Replace 4 cups of the cider with 1 bottle of fruity red wine, like Shiraz, Cabernet Sauvignon, or Merlot. Garnish with lemon rounds instead of the apple.

STAPLES +
MEALTIME
HELPERS

Pressure cookers are brilliant at making all kinds of mealtime helpers, from broths to quick jams, to a super-speedy, fresh-tasting red sauce that easily tops pasta. In this chapter you'll find useful (and mouthwatering!) building blocks that you can stash away, and will get you so much closer to a delicious breakfast or dinner. If you're new to pressure cooking, you'll find that these helpers, perfect for weekend meal prepping, are a great place to start (read: easy payoff). Stock your fridge with these gems and make your life around the table quicker, healthier, and more delicious.

Homemade Yogurt

PREP TIME: 5 MINUTES
TOTAL TIME: 10 HOURS
MAKES ABOUT 8 CUPS
GLUTEN-FREE VEGETARIAN

2 quarts (½ gallon) fresh milk, preferably organic

½ cup heavy cream, preferably organic (optional)

2 tablespoons plain yogurt (with live active cultures; see Cook's Notes)

COOK'S NOTE

A Cleaner Culture: When you're looking for a starter culture (the 2 tablespoons taken from a prepared yogurt) to begin making your own yogurt, look for a high-quality brand of plain, all-natural yogurt (no flavorings or funny business like corn syrup) and one with at least four live active cultures.

COOK'S NOTE

Low-Fat Yogurt: For a slightly reduced fat content, skip the cream or opt for half-and-half and 2 percent milk; however, I don't recommend making this with skim milk, which makes a thin and watery yogurt.

TRY THIS! GREEK YOGURT

For a thicker, Greek-style yogurt, drain the prepared yogurt by spooning it into a colander lined with a double layer of cheesecloth and setting it over a bowl. Refrigerate overnight or until the yogurt reaches your desired consistency. You can use the drained liquid (whey) like buttermilk.

When I first saw the Yogurt button on my new multicooker (older models don't have this feature), I thought I could just pour in some farm fresh milk, press the button, and presto: thick, creamy yogurt. While it's not *quite* that simple, it's not terribly challenging, either, and it's worth the effort because it is far more economical to make yogurt at home than to buy it in the store. You can also guarantee the quality and ingredients and a super-creamy result. If you love cream-top yogurt, adding in a touch of cream will get you there.

A multicooker with a Yogurt function *does* take much of the guesswork out of yogurt making, but do mind the details. The reward for a little extra attention is vats of creamy, healthful yogurt for spooning into and over all your favorite foods. Remember to save 2 tablespoons from your current batch to make your next batch. And flavor your yogurt if you like; see the box on page 161.

1. Pour the milk and cream (if using) into the inner pot of the multicooker. Set to Saute and heat until the milk boils (it should be about 180°F on an instant-read thermometer).

2. Allow the milk to cool to between 105°F and 115°F on the instant-read thermometer, about 1 hour on the countertop or 15 minutes if you set the inner pot into an ice bath. (I make one in my sink, filling the sink with ice cubes and water, and sticking the base of the inner pot right in while stirring the milk to cool it even faster.) Skim and discard any skin that forms on top from the milk.

3. Stir in the prepared yogurt. Return the inner pot to the multicooker (dry the base first if you used an ice bath). Lock on the lid and be sure the steam valve is open. Set the Yogurt function and set the time to 8 hours.

4. Open the lid and cool completely on the countertop. Transfer the yogurt to clean jars or an airtight container and refrigerate for at least 6 hours for the yogurt to set up to the proper consistency before serving. (The yogurt keeps in the refrigerator for up to 10 days.)

Flavored Yogurts

LEMON (OR LIME) YOGURT

In a small bowl, combine 2 teaspoons finely grated lemon zest, 1 tablespoon lemon juice, 1 tablespoon pure maple syrup, and 1 teaspoon cornstarch. Stir to make a smooth paste. When the plain yogurt is finished and chilled, stir the lemon-maple mixture into the yogurt and let the yogurt chill overnight in the fridge. Stir before serving.

MAPLE YOGURT

In a small pot over low heat, reduce ¼ cup pure maple syrup to 2 tablespoons (it will take 5 to 8 minutes). When the plain yogurt is completely cool, stir in the reduced syrup and let the yogurt chill overnight in the fridge. Stir before serving.

VANILLA YOGURT

Add 1 vanilla bean, split in half, to the inner pot along with the milk and cook as directed, then chill overnight in the fridge. Fish out the vanilla bean before serving and sweeten as desired.

Dairy-Free Coconut Yogurt

PREP TIME: 5 MINUTES
TOTAL TIME: 24 HOURS
MAKES 2½ CUPS
GLUTEN-FREE DAIRY-FREE
VEGAN VEGETARIAN*

1 (13.5-ounce) can coconut cream

1 (13.5-ounce) can full-fat coconut milk (not refrigerated coconut milk)

1 tablespoon pure maple syrup or sugar

2 teaspoons unflavored powdered gelatin, or 1 tablespoon agar agar flakes
*For vegan and vegetarian, use agar agar

3 tablespoons prepared nondairy plain yogurt (with live active cultures, see Cook's Notes, page 160)

Sometimes we crave something creamy but nondairy, and since we have plenty of friends who can't have dairy at all, I love having this to offer them. It's also a great plant-based midday snack, easily turned into an *almost-sweet* with the addition of berries and a drizzle of maple syrup. I use a blend of full-fat coconut milk and coconut cream (the thick layer that rises to the top of traditional coconut milk) to get the thickness and mouthfeel of a rich yogurt (using only coconut milk will result in something a bit too runny). You'll need to cook the coconut yogurt for a full 18 to 24 hours to get the thickness you may be used to from commercial yogurts.

1. Pour the coconut cream, coconut milk, and maple syrup into the inner pot of the multicooker, and whisk well. Set on the Saute function and cook until the coconut milk boils and all the coconut solids are fully melted (it should be about 180°F on an instant-read thermometer). Whisk in the gelatin until smooth.

2. Allow the milk to cool to around 105°F on the instant-read thermometer, about 1 hour on the countertop or 15 minutes in an ice bath. (I make one in my sink, filling the sink with ice cubes and water, and sticking the base of the pot right in, stirring frequently to make sure the coconut solids don't set.)

3. Return the inner pot to the multicooker (dry the base first if you used an ice bath). Stir in 2 tablespoons of the prepared yogurt. Lock on the lid and make sure the steam vent is open. Set the Yogurt function to 18 to 24 hours (24 hours for a thicker, creamier yogurt, 18 hours for a runnier version).

4. Open the lid and let cool completely on the countertop. Transfer the yogurt to clean jars or an airtight container. Refrigerate for at least 6 hours before serving so that the yogurt sets up to the proper consistency (gelatin thickens over time).

5. Stir well before serving (to make sure any gelatin that has settled is re-emulsified into the yogurt). Flavor your yogurt as desired, using the suggestions on page 161.

Creamy Homemade Ricotta

PREP TIME: 5 MINUTES
TOTAL TIME: 35 MINUTES
MAKES 1½ CUPS
GLUTEN-FREE VEGETARIAN

6 cups whole milk, preferably organic

¾ cup heavy cream, preferably organic

2 tablespoons lemon juice or distilled white vinegar

½ teaspoon fine sea salt (optional)

I know what you're thinking: homemade ricotta—is that really necessary? Strictly speaking, no. But homemade ricotta is really a game changer. Try it for a ricotta-and-jam toast (see page 48), add a dollop over your Quick Pork Bolognese for a Crowd (*highly* recommended; page 122), or serve a spoonful alongside fresh summer berries. I know you're going to love this looser, curdy homemade kind—similar to the type you find in a high-end grocer or an Italian delicatessen (but often pay dearly for). It's *very* easy to make at home and worth the minuscule effort required. Consider this a non-fussy luxury worth having (or gifting, with a loaf of great bread).

1. Pour the milk and cream into the inner pot of the multicooker, lock on the lid, and be sure the vent is left open. Set the Yogurt function and adjust to Boil.

2. When the Boil cycle is complete, open the lid, add the lemon juice, and stir gently a few times (aggressive stirring can produce grainy results). When the white curds start to separate (about 30 seconds), let the mixture stand undisturbed for 5 minutes.

3. Drain the ricotta in a cheesecloth-lined colander set over a large bowl; this usually takes 5 minutes for a moist ricotta and up to 1 hour for firmer ricotta.

4. Taste the ricotta and season with salt, if desired (I prefer it plain for breakfasts and toasts). Scoop the thickened ricotta out of the cheesecloth, and transfer it to clean jars or an airtight container. Let cool completely, then serve at room temperature, or refrigerate for up to 5 days.

From-Scratch Pumpkin Butter

PREP TIME: 5 MINUTES
TOTAL TIME: 1½ HOURS
MAKES 3 CUPS
GLUTEN-FREE DAIRY-FREE
VEGAN VEGETARIAN

1 small sugar pumpkin or kabocha squash (about 2 pounds), halved crosswise and seeded

⅓ cup apple cider

1 tablespoon coconut oil, melted

⅓ cup pure maple syrup

¼ cup coconut sugar or light or dark brown sugar

2 cinnamon sticks

½ teaspoon fine sea salt

½ teaspoon freshly grated nutmeg

FOR THE SLOW COOKER

Place the pumpkin in the slow cooker and cook for 5 hours on High or 8 hours on Low. Halve and scoop out the pumpkin flesh, then return it to the slow cooker and add the other ingredients. Cook on Low until smooth and thick, about another 2 hours. Then continue with step 4 to cool and puree the butter.

A pressure cooker is brilliant at cooking rock-hard vegetables in a fraction of the usual time. I love cooking pumpkins (any squash, really) into a subtly sweet, spoonable butter that is beautiful on toast (see Perfect Toast, page 48) or pancakes, but it especially shines when dolloped into a bowl of yogurt or served atop your favorite porridge.

1. Place the pumpkin and about 1 cup water in the inner pot of the pressure cooker. Lock on the lid and Pressure Cook on high pressure for 20 minutes. Let the pressure release naturally (about 20 minutes), then open the lid.

2. Remove the pumpkin with a slotted spoon and discard the liquid in the inner pot. Scoop out the pumpkin flesh and return it to the inner pot; discard the skin. Add the cider, coconut oil, maple syrup, sugar, cinnamon sticks, salt, and nutmeg.

3. Lock on the lid again and Pressure Cook on high pressure for 10 minutes. Let the steam release naturally (about 10 minutes), then release any remaining pressure manually.

4. Let stand for 15 minutes, then open the lid. Remove the cinnamon sticks and puree the pumpkin until smooth with an immersion blender or in an upright blender or food processor. Let cool.

5. Spoon the pumpkin puree into clean glass jars with tight-fitting lids or an airtight plastic container. Refrigerate for up to 2 weeks or freeze for up to 2 months; if freezing, make sure to leave plenty of room at the top of the container for the pumpkin butter to expand.

TRY THIS! CHAI-SPICED PUMPKIN BUTTER

The recipe for the pumpkin butter has the traditional spices of cinnamon and nutmeg, but you can add ¼ teaspoon each ground ginger and cardamom and a pinch of ground cloves during the second cooking time for a chai-spiced finish.

Apple-Pear Sauce

PREP TIME: 10 MINUTES
TOTAL TIME: 25 MINUTES
MAKES ABOUT 6 CUPS
GLUTEN-FREE DAIRY-FREE
VEGAN VEGETARIAN

6 large, crisp, tart apples, such as Crispin, Jonagold, Honeycrisp, Ginger Gold, or Pink Lady (about 3 pounds), peeled, cored, and halved

4 large red or green Anjou pears (about 2 pounds), peeled, cored, and halved

2 cinnamon sticks

Pinch of fine sea salt

½ cup apple juice

If there's one thing we make over and over again in our pressure cooker, it's applesauce. We eat it warm for breakfast, on the side for lunch, and spooned over yogurt as an impromptu healthy dessert. It's an absolute cinch to make. McIntosh, a traditional sauce apple, breaks down to mush in the pressure cooker, so I prefer tart, crisp varieties that hold a bit of body and bite. Vary the apple varieties and the ratio of apples to pears to your liking here, or change it a bit every time you make it.

1. Combine the apples, pears, cinnamon sticks, salt, and apple juice in the inner pot of the pressure cooker. Lock on the lid and Pressure Cook on high pressure for 7 minutes. Release the pressure manually and open the lid. Remove the cinnamon sticks.

2. Mash the fruit with a potato masher if you like a chunkier sauce, or blend it with an immersion blender if you prefer a more uniform texture.

3. Serve warm or at room temperature, or cool completely and refrigerate in an airtight container for up to 1 week.

A SAUCE FOR EVERY SEASON

Apple-Plum Sauce:
Use 6 small plums, pitted, in place of the pears.

Double-Cinnamon Applesauce:
Double the cinnamon sticks during cooking, or add an additional ½ teaspoon ground cinnamon to the finished sauce.

Apple-Cranberry Sauce:
Replace the pears with 3 cups fresh cranberries, washed and picked over. Sweeten (after cooking) with up to ¼ cup honey, sugar, or maple syrup.

Raspberry Maple Jam

PREP TIME: 5 MINUTES
TOTAL TIME: 20 MINUTES
MAKES ABOUT 2¼ CUPS
GLUTEN-FREE DAIRY-FREE
VEGAN VEGETARIAN

4 cups fresh or frozen raspberries (see Cook's Note)

2 tablespoons fresh lemon juice

2 to 3 tablespoons pure maple syrup

3 tablespoons chia seeds

COOK'S NOTE

The Best, Brightest Berries Might Be . . . Frozen: Fresh berries work beautifully for this jam, but frozen not only offer a more economical all-season option but often also produce a more vibrantly colored jam. For a different flavor, try substituting 4 cups blackberries.

Raspberry jam is a bright spot in life. I love how it captures the essence of summer, especially when I dip into a jar of it on the dreariest rainy spring day or on a frigid winter morning. Making jam from scratch is an absolute cinch—it's the sterilizing and storing that tend to add angst. So I skip the angst by making quick jams that are kept in the fridge and enjoyed over shorter periods of time.

This recipe uses pressure cooking to quickly release the berries' vibrant juices, maple syrup to sweeten them, and chia seeds to thicken them in an instant, without pectin or loads of sugar. Use this jam for topping yogurt or porridge, or for spreading on thick sourdough toast (especially great with a smear of homemade ricotta; see page 163).

1. Stir the raspberries, lemon juice, 2 tablespoons maple syrup, and the chia seeds together in the inner pot of the pressure cooker. Lock on the lid and Pressure Cook on high pressure for 1 minute, just to release the juices.

2. Let the pressure release naturally (about 10 minutes), then release the remaining pressure manually. Open the lid.

3. Stir the berries lightly to make sure all the chia is absorbed, but not so much that the raspberries completely break down. Transfer the jam to a bowl or jar to cool for 5 to 10 minutes. Once cooled, taste and sweeten with up to 1 tablespoon more maple syrup, if needed. Refrigerate the jam in clean jars or an airtight container for up to 1 month.

TRY THIS! MARMALADE VARIATIONS

You can make marmalade with blood oranges, Cara Cara oranges, or Valencia oranges, all of which have somewhat thicker skins and a more bitter taste but still give deeply pleasing results. Halve and remove the seeds before cooking, and adjust the sweetness to your liking after the pressure cooking.

Whole Mandarin Marmalade

PREP TIME: 10 MINUTES
TOTAL TIME: 55 MINUTES
MAKES 4 HEAPING CUPS
GLUTEN-FREE DAIRY-FREE
VEGAN VEGETARIAN

2 pounds seedless Mandarin oranges, preferably organic and well scrubbed

1 lemon, preferably organic, halved and seeded

2½ cups sugar

Pinch of fine sea salt

I'm a marmalade girl—marmalade on toast, in yogurt, layered in a parfait. I love the big, tangy strips of sweetened but still slightly bitter skin spread on lusciously buttered toast. Making marmalade from scratch is usually a chore—a several-day process that involves peeling the citrus and removing the bitter pith before slicing the peel into thin strips. What I like about making it myself is that I can have it exactly how I want it—I prefer a looser, chunkier marmalade, which can be hard to find and expensive. So here's the good news: a 2-pound bag of Mandarin oranges (thin-skinned and seedless) is a breeze to chop and cook into three glorious jars of tangy jam in under an hour. This version is *not* light on the sugar—it's required both to thicken the juices and to balance the bitterness of the skin—but it's a special treat. Life will never be the same.

1. Remove any stems and cut the Mandarins in half (skin and flesh). Slice into thin half-moons or roughly chop.

2. Add the Mandarins to the inner pot of the pressure cooker along with the lemon halves, 2 cups of the sugar, and the salt. Lock on the lid and Pressure Cook on high pressure for 10 minutes to release the juices and soften the skins. Release the pressure manually.

3. Open the lid and stir in the remaining ½ cup sugar. Set to the Saute function and continue cooking until the liquid evaporates and the marmalade thickens, 20 to 25 minutes, stirring occasionally.

4. Remove the lemon halves and let the marmalade cool completely at room temperature. Transfer to clean jars or an airtight container and store in the fridge for up to 1 month.

All the Pickled Vegetables

PREP TIME: 10 MINUTES
TOTAL TIME: 25 MINUTES
MAKES ABOUT 2 PINTS
GLUTEN-FREE DAIRY-FREE
VEGAN VEGETARIAN

2 cups distilled white vinegar or apple cider vinegar

¼ cup sugar

2 tablespoons pickling spices, such as whole cloves, allspice berries, black peppercorns, or mustard seeds

2 bay leaves

1½ tablespoons kosher salt

1 or 2 sprigs fresh herbs, such as dill, rosemary, or cilantro, plus more for serving

1½ pounds fresh vegetables, trimmed, such as whole green beans, cauliflower florets, small carrots, or pickling cucumbers, halved lengthwise

This is a reminder that just about any vegetable—from cucumbers to beets to cauliflower—can be pickled quickly and used to brighten up otherwise humdrum meals. What you're doing here is making a super-fast but potent pickling liquid (a strong brine) in the pressure cooker, then pouring it over cleaned and trimmed vegetables that have been packed into glass jars. The pickling happens fast in the intimate quarters of the jars, with a little extra time to cure in the refrigerator. Use this quick-pickling trick throughout the seasons (if opting for beets, steam and peel them first, using the method described on page 94).

1. Combine 8 cups water with the vinegar, sugar, pickling spices, bay leaves, salt, and herbs in the inner pot of the pressure cooker. Lock on the lid and Pressure Cook on high pressure for 7 minutes. Release the pressure manually and open the lid.

2. Pack the vegetables into two clean 1-pint canning jars or airtight containers and fill with the brine, leaving ½ inch of headspace. Discard the extra brine (or use it to quickly pickle a sliced red onion).

3. Let the jars cool completely before refrigerating for up to 1 month. Serve cold or at room temperature, adding fresh-chopped herbs, if desired, before serving.

TRY THIS! SPICY PICKLED VEGETABLES

For a little heat in your pickle, add 1 jalapeño pepper, sliced in rounds, to the pickling liquid before cooking.

Quick Pomodoro Sauce

PREP TIME: 10 MINUTES
TOTAL TIME: 40 MINUTES
MAKES ABOUT 6½ CUPS
GLUTEN-FREE DAIRY-FREE*
VEGAN* VEGETARIAN

3 tablespoons extra-virgin
 olive oil

2 garlic cloves, smashed or sliced

Generous pinch of red pepper
 flakes

2 (28-ounce) cans whole San
 Marzano tomatoes

½ teaspoon fine sea salt, plus
 more as needed

1 sprig of fresh basil (optional)

1 bay leaf

Freshly ground black pepper

2 tablespoons unsalted butter,
 plus more as needed *For
 dairy-free and vegan, omit or
 use dairy-free butter

COOK'S NOTE

Arrabbiata Sauce: Double the red
pepper flakes for a spicier finish!

This in-a-flash fresh tomato sauce can serve many purposes. It's a quick solution for weeknight dinners, served with pasta that's cooked right in the sauce (see variation that follows), as a starting point for Easy Eggplant Parmesan (page 108), as an easy sauce for pizza; or as a poaching bed for eggs (see Breakfast Shakshuka, page 31). Because the sauce is cooked fast under pressure, it remains looser than a marinara or a jarred pasta sauce. I love its fresh, sun-ripened-tomato taste and its big, chunky pieces of tomato (that's why I always start with canned whole tomatoes, never diced). If you want something thicker, simmer on the Saute setting for up to 15 minutes after opening the lid.

1. Pour the oil into the inner pot of the pressure cooker and set to the Saute function. Add the garlic and red pepper flakes and cook until fragrant, stirring constantly, 1 minute.

2. Carefully add the tomatoes and their juices (they may splatter as they hit the hot oil), crushing them with your hands as you add them to the pot. Add the ½ teaspoon salt, basil (if using), and bay leaf and stir. Lock on the lid and Pressure Cook on high pressure for 5 minutes, or until the sauce thickens. Release the pressure manually and open the lid. Remove and discard the basil sprig and bay leaf.

3. Taste the sauce and add more salt, if needed, and some pepper; stir to combine. Use a potato masher to crush the tomatoes, pressing lightly for a chunkier sauce (my preference) or firmly for a smoother sauce. Stir in the butter (to soften the acidity of the tomatoes) and serve warm. Or cool completely and refrigerate in an airtight container for up to 1 week.

TRY THIS! ONE-POT PASTA DINNER

This one-pot pasta dish eliminates the need to cook the pasta separately, making cleanup a breeze! Combine 5 cups Quick Pomodoro Sauce (warm or at room temperature) with 12 ounces uncooked long and thin pasta, such as linguine or spaghetti, broken in half. Stir several times to ensure the pasta is coated with sauce and isn't sticking together. Lock on the lid and Pressure Cook on high pressure for 4 minutes. Let the pressure release naturally (about 16 minutes), then open the lid. Stir well to soften all the noodles into the sauce, and serve in bowls or on plates, with a generous sprinkling of parmesan.

Potent Vegetable Broth

PREP TIME: 10 MINUTES
TOTAL TIME: 50 MINUTES
MAKES 3 QUARTS
GLUTEN-FREE DAIRY-FREE
VEGAN VEGETARIAN

1 medium onion, quartered

4 large carrots, thickly sliced

4 celery stalks, chopped, plus
   some leaves

1 medium fennel bulb, halved

2 garlic cloves, halved

3 bay leaves

1 teaspoon coriander seeds

6 whole black peppercorns

3 sprigs of fresh thyme

3 sprigs of fresh parsley

2 teaspoons fine sea salt

1 tablespoon harissa or
   Hungarian hot paprika paste
   (optional)

FOR THE SLOW COOKER

Combine all the ingredients in the slow cooker and cook on High for 3 hours. Strain and continue to step 3.

If anyone in your family is vegetarian or vegan, you'll need a flavorful vegetable broth for stews, risottos, and so much more. I've yet to find a prepared (boxed) vegetable broth worth the trouble of going to the store for, especially when a fragrant, deeply flavorful homemade version is virtually effortless. And chances are that most of the ingredients are already in your fridge or vegetable bin.

For deeper flavor and a touch of heat, I like to work in a tablespoon of hot paprika paste or harissa. And when I have them, fresh or dried mushrooms add tone and body (see Mushroom Broth, which follows). You can get a light and usable vegetable broth in just 30 minutes, but I recommend the full 40 minutes for a full-bodied, rich-flavored broth.

1. Place the onion, carrots, celery, fennel, garlic, bay leaves, coriander seeds, peppercorns, thyme and parsley sprigs, salt, and harissa (if using) in the inner pot of the pressure cooker. Add the water, taking care not to surpass the maximum fill line.

2. Lock on the lid and Pressure Cook on high pressure for 40 minutes. Release the steam naturally to deepen flavors (about 20 minutes), then open the lid. Strain the broth through a colander lined with cheesecloth and discard the solids. Return the broth to the inner pot and leave on the Keep Warm setting until ready to use.

3. To store, cool the broth completely and refrigerate in an airtight container for up to 1 week; or freeze for up to 3 months, leaving 1 inch of headspace for expansion.

TRY THIS! MUSHROOM BROTH
(GLUTEN-FREE DAIRY-FREE VEGAN VEGETARIAN)

Prepare as for the vegetable broth, but add 8 ounces dried shiitake mushrooms or 12 ounces of fresh shiitakes (brushed clean and chopped) and 2 tablespoons soy sauce. After cooking, ladle the broth into a large bowl rather than straining it; mushrooms often harbor grit or sand that should be left at the bottom of the pot.

Beef Bone Broth, Pho Style

PREP TIME: 15 MINUTES
TOTAL TIME: 2 HOURS
MAKES 3 QUARTS BROTH,
ABOUT 4 CUPS COOKED MEAT
GLUTEN-FREE DAIRY-FREE

2 pounds beef shin bones, cut into 2-inch lengths (ask the butcher), or meaty oxtails

2 pounds beef short ribs, or boneless chuck roast, cut into 1-inch pieces

2 teaspoons fine sea salt, plus more as needed

Freshly ground black pepper

2 small onions, quartered

4 garlic cloves, sliced

4 celery stalks, sliced, with some leaves roughly chopped

1 teaspoon whole cloves

1 tablespoon coriander seeds

1 tablespoon fennel seeds (optional)

2 tablespoons coconut sugar or dark brown sugar

FOR THE SLOW COOKER

Combine the ingredients in a slow cooker and cook on High for 6 hours.

TRY THIS!
LAMB BONE BROTH

Prepare as for the beef broth, substituting 2 (1¼-pound) lamb shanks for the beef.

A dark, deep-toned beef broth is a wonderfully versatile base for soups, stews, and risottos when you need that extra oomph. A wide variety of beef cuts or bones will work, but I love a combination of shin bones and chuck, or even oxtails. (Likewise, you can make a similarly rich lamb broth—see the variation that follows.) This rich beef broth is akin to the broth that serves as the base for *pho*, a very popular Vietnamese beef-noodle soup that I learned to make from food writer Andrea Nguyen. It's so delicious you could drink it on its own. The cooked meat that results here can be saved for Traditional Beef Borscht (page 72) or Brothy Beef Stew (page 75).

1. Place the bones and meat in the inner pot of the pressure cooker and season with 2 teaspoons salt and some pepper. Set to the Saute function and brown the meat and bones, about 12 minutes, turning as needed (it's okay if not all sides are browned; the surface area of the pot is small for this).

2. Add the onions, garlic, celery, cloves, coriander and fennel seeds, and about 8 cups water for a 6-quart pressure cooker or about 9 cups for an 8-quart cooker. The water should *just meet* the maximum fill line (if necessary, remove a little water). Add the sugar.

3. Lock on the lid and Pressure Cook on high pressure for 90 minutes. Release the steam naturally (about 20 minutes), then release manually (the flavors will deepen as the broth sits).

4. Open the lid and skim the fat from the broth. Fish out and discard the bones. Remove the meat and let cool. Store the meat in an airtight container in the fridge for up to 3 days or freeze for up to 1 month.

5. Strain the broth, discarding the solids. Season with additional salt, if needed. Let cool completely, then refrigerate in airtight containers for up to 1 week or freeze (leaving 1 inch of headroom for expansion) for up to 3 months.

Duck or Pork Bone Broth

PREP TIME: 15 MINUTES
TOTAL TIME: 1 HOUR 30 MINUTES
MAKES ABOUT 13 CUPS BROTH,
7 CUPS COOKED MEAT
GLUTEN-FREE DAIRY-FREE

1 (5-pound) Peking or Rohan duck, or 1 (4-pound) bone-in pork shoulder

2 teaspoons fine sea salt

1 teaspoon freshly ground black pepper

2 leeks, cleaned and thickly sliced

2 large carrots, sliced

4 celery stalks, sliced and some leaves chopped

2 bay leaves

FOR THE SLOW COOKER

Place all ingredients in a slow cooker and cook on Low for 8 to 10 hours.

A good duck or pork broth is a rich and deeply flavorful tool to have in your cooking arsenal. But both duck and pork need to be treated a little differently, owing to their high fat content—they both require a bit more skimming. The results are magnificent, though: fortifying as a cold-weather remedy and truly remarkable as a base for the richer recipes in this book. Their cooking treatments are basically the same, so they are combined here.

1. Season the duck or pork with the salt and pepper.

2. Place the leeks in the inner pot of the pressure cooker and place the duck or pork on top. If using duck, tuck in the legs so it fits snugly on its backbone without crossing the maximum fill line.

3. Tuck the carrots, celery, and bay leaves all around and cover with 8 cups water for a 6-quart pressure cooker and 9 cups for an 8-quart cooker; the water should *just meet* the fill line (if necessary, remove some of the water).

4. Lock on the lid and Pressure Cook on high pressure for 50 minutes. Release the pressure manually.

5. Open the lid and skim the fat from the broth. Remove the duck or pork and let cool. Then pull the meat from the bones, discarding the skin and bones. Pack into an airtight container and refrigerate for up to 3 days, or store it in a resealable bag and freeze for up to 1 month.

6. Strain the broth through a cheesecloth-lined colander, discarding the solids. Let cool completely, then refrigerate in airtight containers for up to 1 week; or freeze for up to 3 months (leave 1 inch of headroom for expansion if freezing).

Double-Duty Poached Chicken and Chicken Broth

PREP TIME: 15 MINUTES
TOTAL TIME: 1 HOUR
MAKES 2½ QUARTS BROTH,
7 CUPS COOKED CHICKEN
GLUTEN-FREE DAIRY-FREE

1 (3- to 4-pound) roasting chicken

2 teaspoons fine sea salt

1 teaspoon freshly ground black pepper

1 large onion, quartered

1 head garlic, halved crosswise

2 large carrots, sliced

4 celery stalks, sliced, plus some leaves

2 bay leaves

8 to 10 cups water

1 teaspoon coriander seeds

6 whole black peppercorns

3 sprigs of fresh thyme

3 sprigs of fresh parsley

FOR THE SLOW COOKER

Place the seasonings, chicken, and water in the slow cooker and cook on Low for 10 hours.

TRY THIS! GINGER-SESAME CHICKEN BROTH
(GLUTEN-FREE DAIRY-FREE)

For congee (see page 36), try making a Chinese-style chicken broth. Replace the onion, carrots, and celery with 1 peeled knob of fresh ginger, 3 scallions cut in half lengthwise. Finish with 3 teaspoons toasted sesame or peanut oil.

In the heat of busy family life, there's no point making broth that doesn't do double duty, getting you *even* closer to your next great meal. That's why I love using a plump whole roasting bird for making broth. It yields a flavorful broth, as well as over 2 pounds of juicy, succulent meat. Shred the meat and use it to stuff sweet potatoes (see page 109), top congee (see page 36), or make a chicken salad. Or serve the chicken along with soft-boiled eggs atop a Greek salad. The uses are endless.

1. Season the skin and cavity of the chicken with the salt and pepper.

2. Place the onion in the inner pot of the pressure cooker and set the chicken on top, tucking in its legs and wings so it fits snugly on its backbone without crossing the pot's maximum fill line.

3. Tuck the garlic, carrots, celery, and bay leaves all around the chicken. Cover with 8 cups water for a 6-quart pressure cooker or about 10 cups for an 8-quart pressure cooker. The water level should *just meet* the maximum fill line (if necessary, remove some of the water).

4. Lock on the lid and Pressure Cook on high pressure for 25 minutes. Release the steam manually and open the lid. Remove the chicken from the pot and let cool briefly.

5. Strain the broth through a cheesecloth-lined colander, discarding all the solids. Let the broth cool completely.

6. Pull the chicken meat from the bones, discarding the skin and bones. Shred or chop the meat for future use: pack it in an airtight container in the refrigerator for up to 3 days, or freeze in a resealable bag for 1 month.

7.   Refrigerate the broth in airtight containers for up to 1 week, or freeze it (leaving 1 inch of headspace for expansion) for up to 3 months.

APPENDIX: PRESSURE COOKER COOKING CHARTS

Given an hour or two on the weekend and your pressure cooker by your side, preparing the building blocks for faster, healthier, more satisfying meals has never been easier. Use these charts as guides for pressure cooking your basic batches of beans, grains, rice, vegetables, and meats.

Refer to the charts for the suggested pressure-release method, either MR/QR (manual or quick release) or NR (natural release). Bear in mind that the natural release can take anywhere from 10 minutes to over an hour, depending on how full the pot is.

DRIED BEANS

The pressure cooker offers the option of cooking dried beans directly, but for even cooking and beans that best hold their shape, it is recommended you soak the beans prior to cooking (some believe this also makes beans easier to digest, since the soaking liquid is poured off). The pressure cooker also offers the option of a quick-soak: instead of soaking the dried beans for several hours, you can pressure-soak them in the cooker for 2 minutes to get them started.

OVERNIGHT SOAK: Soak 1 pound dried beans in 8 cups fresh water for 10 to 12 hours.

QUICK-SOAK: Place 1 pound dried beans, 8 cups water, and 2 teaspoons salt in the pressure cooker. Pressure Cook on high pressure for 2 minutes, then use the natural release.

PRESSURE COOK: Drain and rinse the soaked beans and add them to the pressure cooker with 6 cups fresh water. Pressure Cook using the times indicated below. (I like to cook beans with a bit of salt—with more to be added later—½ onion, and 1 bay leaf or, if I have it on hand, a sheet of konbu seaweed, which makes the beans more digestible and helps tenderize them; just fish out the konbu after cooking.)

This chart assumes 1 pound of dried beans (for rice, beans, and other foods that expand, never fill your pot beyond half full).

COOK'S NOTE: For an extra measure of success when cooking chickpeas, add 1 teaspoon baking soda to your soaking liquid and another to your cooking liquid, which helps break down the outer casing and yields a creamier center.

BEAN TYPE	PRESSURE RELEASE	COOKING TIME FOR SOAKED BEANS (S) & UNSOAKED BEANS (U)
		5 · 10 · 15 · 20 · 25 · 30 (# minutes)
Black	NR	10–15 (S) / 20–25 (U)
Black-Eyed Peas	NR	10–15 (S) / 14–18 (U)
Flageolet	NR	10–15 (S) / 20–25 (U)
Pinto	NR	9–15 (S) / 25–30 (U)
Pinquito	NR	10–15 (S) / 20–25 (U)
Red	NR	10–15 (S) / 20–25 (U)
Cannellini	NR	15–20 (S) / 25–30
Chickpeas (Garbanzos)	NR	20–25 (S) / 25–30 (U)
Corona or Gigantes	NR	20–25 (S) / 25–30 (U)
Great Northern	NR	20–25 (S) / 25–30 (U)
Kidney	NR	20–25 (S) / 25–30 (U)
Navy	NR	20–25 (S) / 25–30 (U)

LENTILS

Lentils are not generally soaked prior to cooking. Pick over and rinse the lentils. Add the lentils to the inner pot of the pressure cooker along with 2½ cups water and ½ teaspoon sea salt, using the times indicated below. The cooking time is shorter for firmer lentils (for salads) and longer for lentils that break down more fully (for soups and dals).

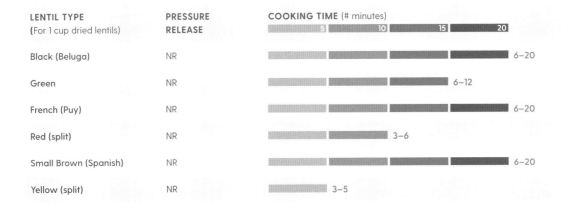

LENTIL TYPE (For 1 cup dried lentils)	PRESSURE RELEASE	COOKING TIME (# minutes)
		5 · 10 · 15 · 20
Black (Beluga)	NR	6–20
Green	NR	6–12
French (Puy)	NR	6–20
Red (split)	NR	3–6
Small Brown (Spanish)	NR	6–20
Yellow (split)	NR	3–5

RICE AND OTHER GRAINS

Best practice is to soak rice in water for 15 minutes before cooking and then rinse until the water runs clear; soaking for at least 15 minutes is said to reduce trace toxins (see Cook's Note, page 102). If you decide to skip the soaking, add up to ¼ cup extra water with the rice before cooking (except for the congee, which is already cooked in copious liquid).

Other grains do not need to be soaked. Place the grains in the inner pot of the pressure cooker, add water as indicated on page 183, and Pressure Cook following the times indicated.

For rice and grains that are fluffy and separate rather than clumped and gummy, open the lid after cooking, drape a clean kitchen towel over the inner pot, and re-cover with the lid slightly ajar. The towel will absorb excess moisture while the rice finishes steaming. Fluff the rice with a fork before serving.

For rice, beans, and foods that expand, never fill your pot beyond half full.

GRAIN TYPE	LIQUID FOR 1 CUP GRAIN	PRESSURE RELEASE	COOKING TIME (minutes)
			5 10 15 20 25 30
Barley, pearled	1⅓–2 cups	NR for 10 minutes, then MR/QR	25–30
Couscous (not quick-cooking)	2 cups	NR for 10 minutes, then MR/QR	5–8
Millet	1⅔ cups	NR for 10 minutes, then MR/QR	10–12
Oats (old-fashioned)	1⅔ cups	NR for 10 minutes, then MR/QR	6
Oats (steel-cut)	3 cups	NR for 10 minutes, then MR/QR	10–12
Polenta (coarse)	4 cups	NR for 10 minutes, then MR/QR	10–15
Porridge	5–6 cups	NR for 10 minutes, then MR/QR	15–20
Rice (for congee)	4–5 cups	NR for 10 minutes, then MR/QR	15–20
Rice, long-grain (basmati or jasmine)	1 cup (soaked) / 1¼ cups (unsoaked)	NR for 10 minutes, then MR/QR	4–8
Rice, short-grain brown	1 cup (soaked) / 1¼ cups (unsoaked)	NR for 10 minutes, then MR/QR	20–25
Rice, long-grain brown (basmati)	1 cup (soaked) / 1¼ cups (unsoaked)	NR for 10 minutes, then MR/QR	20–22
Rice, white	1 cup (soaked) / 1¼ cups (unsoaked)	NR for 10 minutes, then MR/QR	4–8
Rice, wild	1 cup (soaked) / 1¼ cups (unsoaked)	NR for 10 minutes, then MR/QR	25–30
Spelt, farro, kamut, or wheat berries	1¼ to 2 cups	NR for 10 minutes, then MR/QR	25–30
Amaranth	1 cup	NR for 10 minutes, then MR/QR	5
Quinoa	1¼ cups	NR for 10 minutes, then MR/QR	1

MEAT AND POULTRY

Cooking times will vary depending on the size of the cut of meat (time reference is per pound of meat) and the temperature of the meat at the start (cold versus room temperature).

Never attempt to cook frozen or partially frozen meat, poultry, or seafood in a pressure cooker—it won't cook through evenly and could be dangerous to consume.

MEAT	PRESSURE RELEASE	COOKING TIME PER POUND (# minutes)
		15 / 30 / 45 / 60
Beef, boneless stew meat	NR	25–30
Beef, boneless pot roast or brisket (up to 4 pounds)	NR	36–40
Beef short ribs	NR	30–35
Beef shanks	NR	30–35
Lamb shanks	NR	45–50
Lamb, boneless stew meat	NR	20–25
Pork, butt/shoulder (up to 4 pounds)	NR	45–50
Pork, spare ribs, baby back	NR	20–25
Chicken breast (bone-in)	MR/QR	10–15
Chicken breast (boneless, skinless)	MR/QR	6–8
Chicken parts (bone-in)	MR/QR	15
Chicken thighs (bone-in)	MR/QR	15
Chicken thighs (boneless)	MR/QR	10
Chicken, whole	MR/QR	20–25
Turkey breast (whole, bone-in)	MR/QR	25–30
Turkey leg or drumstick	MR/QR	15–20

FISH AND SEAFOOD

Cooking fresh fish and seafood in the pressure cooker ensures a quick cooking time (no dry outsides with undercooked middles). Always use manual or quick release to release the pressure quickly (waiting for natural release could overcook these smaller, more tender proteins).

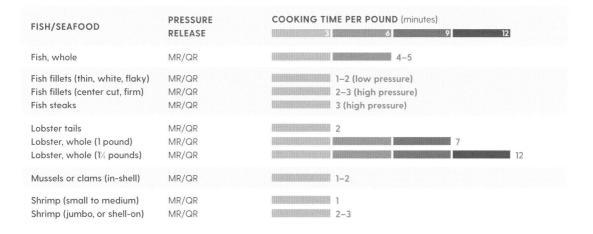

FISH/SEAFOOD	PRESSURE RELEASE	COOKING TIME PER POUND (minutes)
Fish, whole	MR/QR	4–5
Fish fillets (thin, white, flaky)	MR/QR	1–2 (low pressure)
Fish fillets (center cut, firm)	MR/QR	2–3 (high pressure)
Fish steaks	MR/QR	3 (high pressure)
Lobster tails	MR/QR	2
Lobster, whole (1 pound)	MR/QR	7
Lobster, whole (1½ pounds)	MR/QR	12
Mussels or clams (in-shell)	MR/QR	1–2
Shrimp (small to medium)	MR/QR	1
Shrimp (jumbo, or shell-on)	MR/QR	2–3

EGGS AND EGG DISHES

Eggs cook super quickly in a pressure cooker. The cooker also provides a controlled water bath for cooking flans, custards, and puddings. Unless otherwise noted, always use manual or quick release to release the steam pressure, and open the lid quickly (waiting for natural release could overcook these smaller, more tender proteins). Watch each recipe closely for instructions as to whether to cook on low pressure (for soft-boiled eggs, eggs en cocotte, and some custards, like flan) or high pressure (for pudding or quiche).

EGG PREPARATION	PRESSURE RELEASE	COOKING TIME (minutes)
Eggs, soft-boiled	MR/QR	5
Eggs, hard-boiled	MR/QR	6–7
Eggs, poached	MR/QR	5–6
Eggs, baked (en cocotte)	MR/QR	5–6
Egg, in custard (flan, pudding, or quiche)	NR	18–20

VEGETABLES

Most vegetables can be cooked in a pressure cooker in a fraction of the time they would take on the stovetop. Though this chart isn't exhaustive, use the ranges as a guide to cooking most common vegetables.

For this time chart, assume you're filling your pot less than half full and using 1 cup water to create steam. Pressure cooking time is determined by the food's size, not its quantity, so if it takes 12 to 15 minutes to cook one large potato, it will still take 12 to 15 minutes to cook four large potatoes. But adding more to your pressure cooker does increase overall volume in the pot, which will require greater time for the pot to pressurize and depressurize.

If you're starting with frozen vegetables, add 1 to 2 minutes to the cooking time.

VEGETABLE	PRESSURE RELEASE	COOKING TIME PER POUND (minutes)
		7　　14　　21　　28
Asparagus	MR/QR	1–2
Beans, yellow or green	MR/QR	1–2
Artichokes, whole, trimmed	MR/QR	9–11
Artichokes, hearts	MR/QR	4–5
Beets, small whole	NR	11–13
Beets, large whole	NR	20–25
Broccoli, florets	MR/QR	1–2
Brussels sprouts, whole	MR/QR	2–3
Cabbage, wedges	MR/QR	2–3
Carrots, whole or chunks	MR/QR	6–8
Cauliflower, florets	MR/QR	2–3
Corn, on the cob, shucked	MR/QR	3–4
Corn kernels	MR/QR	1–2

VEGETABLE	PRESSURE RELEASE	COOKING TIME PER POUND (minutes)
		7 14 21 28
Eggplant, slices or chunks	MR/QR	2–3
Escarole, chopped	MR/QR	1–2
Greens (collards, kale, spinach, or chard)	MR/QR	3–6
Parsnips, chunks	MR/QR	2–4
Peas, sugar snap (whole)	MR/QR	1–2
Peas, English (shelled)	MR/QR	1–2
Potatoes, chunks	MR/QR	3–5
Potatoes, whole small	MR/QR	8–12
Potatoes, whole large	NR	12–15
Pumpkin, chunks	MR/QR	1–2
Rutabaga, chunks	NR	4–6
Celery root, whole or halved	NR	20–25
Spinach	MR/QR	1–2
Squash (butternut), chunks	MR/QR	4–6
Squash (acorn, delicata, dumpling), halved	NR	15
Squash (spaghetti), halved	NR	15–20
Sweet potatoes, chunks	MR/QR	1–2
Sweet potatoes, whole small	NR	12–15
Sweet potatoes, whole large	NR	15–20

SPECIAL DIETS INDEX

ONE POT MEALS + MAINS

Page	Recipe	GLUTEN-FREE	DAIRY-FREE	VEGAN	VEGETARIAN
107	Cacio e Pepe Risotto	●			○
108	Easy Eggplant Parmesan	●			○
109	Stuffed Sweet Potato "Tacos"	●			○
111	Chicken Tikka Masala	●	●	○	
112	Stovetop-Style Mac 'n' Cheese				○
115	Red Curry Shrimp with Basil and Lime	●	●		
116	Coconut Salmon with Fresh Herbs and Lime	●	●		
119	Mussels in White Wine with Spaghetti				
120	Saucy Chicken and Olives with Greens	●	●		
121	Moroccan Spiced Chicken and Rice	●			
122	Quick Pork Bolognese for a Crowd				
125	Pulled Pork Tacos	●			
126	Simple Saag Paneer	●			○
129	Double-the-Vegetables Pot Roast	●			

SIMPLE DESSERTS

Page	Recipe	GLUTEN-FREE	DAIRY-FREE	VEGAN	VEGETARIAN
134	Stewed Cinnamon Plums	●	●	○	○
137	Deep Dark Chocolate Pudding	●			○
138	Easy Caramel Flan	●			○
140	Vanilla and Cardamom Poached Pears	●	●	○	○
141	Salted Dulce de Leche	●			○
142	Summer Berry Crumble	●	●	○	○
145	Double Chocolate Cheesecake				○
147	Double Citrus Cheesecake				○

COZY DRINKS

Page	Recipe	GLUTEN-FREE	DAIRY-FREE	VEGAN	VEGETARIAN
151	Instant Nut Milk	●	●	○	○
153	French Hot Chocolate	●			○
154	Golden Milk (Turmeric) Latte	●	●	○	○
156	Homemade Chai Masala	●			○
157	Spiced Cider	●	●	○	○

STAPLES + MEALTIME HELPERS

Page	Recipe	GLUTEN-FREE	DAIRY-FREE	VEGAN	VEGETARIAN
160	Homemade Yogurt	●			○
162	Dairy-Free Coconut Yogurt	●	●	○	○
163	Creamy Homemade Ricotta	●			○
165	From-Scratch Pumpkin Butter	●	●	○	○
166	Apple-Pear Sauce	●	●	○	○
167	Raspberry Maple Jam	●	●	○	○
169	Whole Mandarin Marmalade	●	●	○	○
170	All the Pickled Vegetables	●	●	○	○
173	Quick Pomodoro Sauce	●	●	○	○
174	Potent Vegetable Broth	●	●	○	○
176	Beef Bone Broth, Pho Style	●	●		
177	Duck or Pork Bone Broth	●	●		
178	Double-Duty Poached Chicken and Chicken Broth	●	●		

Acknowledgments

Every book project takes a village, but this one, more than ever, required the help and contribution of so many friends, neighbors, colleagues, and family.

To my editor, Raquel Pelzel, you are a tremendous partner—a huge thank-you for the opportunity to work together. To the whole team at Clarkson Potter, thank you for seeing all this project could be. Kari Stuart, thank you for reminding me to take risks and work outside of my comfort zone.

To the most superstar testing team, without whom this book would not be possible—thank you: Brooke Campbell, Melody Moore, Angie Peccini, Gemma Saylor, Diane Reeder, Tim Copeland, Kristin Ferwerda, Lily O'Dare, Libby Bonahoom Robinson, Fríða Kristinsdóttir, Jennifer Mayser, Thea Hanley, Heather Hirsch, Emily Steel, Katherine Roberts, Jill Keefe, Curt Kalousek, Corrine Cecil, Patrick Bostwick, Jaime Zins Gazes, Carrie Boucher, Sarah Paradoski, Kathleen Lewandowski, Marjon Ames Zimmerman. You fed your families and friends on these recipes and in turn made the end results so much better.

Maya Kardas, thank you for appearing just when I needed you most. Brenda Puchot Jolicoeur, you are an angel from heaven. Griselda Mejia and Yanira Villeda, thank you, always—I couldn't do this without you. Chris Lanier, thank you for having my back on this and so many other projects. To Jonathan Milder, thank you for your astute and careful eye.

To Chris Testani, you are a dream to work with; I can't wait for our next projects. To Michael Carbone and Lorie Reilly, thank you for the great company, good music, and many laughs.

My heartfelt thanks to Hetty McKinnon, Tien Ho, Kay Chun, Judy Kim, and so many others for educating me and illuminating our industry with your time and your talents. Enormous thanks to Doris Josovitz of Lost Quarry for creating such a stunning collection of ceramics just for us; I adore them—and you.

To Rebecca Thuss, thank you for your ever willingness to share. Thanks to Sean Dimin from Sea to Table for the stunning salmon and to Gourmet Sweet Botanicals for sending delicate herbs and greens to upstate New York in the dead of winter. Thank you to Anthropologie for sending beautiful linens and plates to enliven these pages.

To our neighbors Rob and Jane Brundage and Kim and Danny Potocki, for your enthusiasm for and support of my work and for always lending a hand in so many ways to make shooting in our home possible—thank you.

To my dear friends, big and small, who came and ate with me to make the photos in this book even more beautiful: Natalie, Josh, and Jude Livingston; Normann Prince and Scarlett Fillippa Björk Søgaard; McKenna, Jackson, and Cora Potocki—I love seeing your faces (and hands) on these pages.

Greta and Mátyás, I couldn't have dreamed up two better kitchen companions. Thank you for your endless enthusiasm, your beautiful cheerfulness, and for all the nights and days you played quietly, tiptoeing around deadlines and stacks of fragile plates while I wrote and shot this book. András, you continue to show up again and again for these all-consuming projects and to help me see the other side of the finish line, even when I can't. I couldn't do any of this without you.

To all who have supported my previous books, who have cooked or shared my recipes, and who spread the word about my work—endless thank-yous. It is you who keep me going.

And to all parents, grandparents, and caregivers everywhere who do the most selfless thing, feeding the ones you love—bravo! Keep going—your work and your efforts matter, and I see you. This book is for you.

Index